Advance Praise

"'The Gathering Girl' by Amanda Rush is a family memoir that does not settle for easy redemption. In it she collects the fragments of her broken family, studying photographs for body language and facial expressions and pondering artifacts from the past such as toys, shards of stained glass, gifts and artistic doodles that act as unconscious guides. These gatherings take her past leaden words like 'schizophrenic' or 'manic' for her mother and 'alcoholic' or 'adulterer' for her father to a more nuanced view. What she discovers does not repair her family, but it does allow her to acknowledge the sorrow, see the thwarted love there, and forgive her parents and herself. This gathering is a gift for all who seek solace from a troubled past."

—Steven Harvey, author of "The Book of Knowledge and Wonder"

"Amanda Rush's 'The Gathering Girl' is a lyrical meditation on memory and how we become who we are. Amanda takes readers on a sometimes dazzling, sometimes heartbreaking journey to unravel the mystery that was her family. And as Amanda searches the artifacts of her life for answers, she gives voice to the yearning so many of us feel to understand the forces that shaped us. This is a beautiful, surprising book about one woman finding her way home."

—Kate Hopper, author of "Ready for Air" and "Use Your Words"

"A rich accumulation of memory and reflection, 'The Gathering Girl' models ways to explore the past to resolve uncertainties we carry within us. Its images invite us to interrogate albums of our own and determine how well we understand what we're viewing. An honest and insightful memoir."

—Robert Root, author of "Happenstance" and "Lineage"

"Biographers must necessarily comb through what remains but what if the evidence, the boxes and papers and material of a lived life, is one's own? This is memoir as archive, as excavation, as a puzzle box that is its own solution. 'The Gathering Girl' is filled with process, with construction, with recollection, with the resonant pumping of blood. As a reconstruction it is fascinating; as a book it is astounding."

—Christian Kiefer, author of "The Heart of It All"

"'The Gathering Girl' is a tour de force memoir that brings 1970s and 1980s Florida and Ohio to life. Amanda Rush carefully observes family photos, letters, and other artifacts to reconstruct the chaos and beauty that constellate her early life. Her gathering brings us to the heart of where memory both falters and shines to come to terms with the present. 'What matters is what suffering makes of us; what we make of it,' she writes. Amanda's wise and compassionate rendering of the past makes this book unforgettable."

—Sandra Simonds, author of "Triptychs"

"Amanda Rush's 'The Gathering Girl' is a beautiful work of memoir—thoughtful, evocative and bracingly honest about a lifetime's loss and heartbreak. In crystalline, considered prose, Amanda tells us about being a daughter of complex, flawed parents without a hint of sensationalism or grievance. This is a terrific book, clear-eyed and wise. I loved it.

—Christopher Coake, author of "You Would Have Told Me Not To"

The Gathering Girl

Amanda Irene Rush

THE GATHERING GIRL

© Copyright 2023 Amanda Irene Rush

This book is memoir. It reflects the author's present recollections of experiences over time. Some names and characteristics may have been changed, some events may have been compressed, and some dialogue may have been recreated.

Company and/or product names referenced in this book may be logos, trade names, trademarks, and/or registered trademarks, and are the property of their respective owners.

ISBN: 979-8-9865220-7-4 (Softcover)
ISBN: 978-1-962457-26-2 (E-book)
Printed in the United States of America
First Printing: 2023

Published by Publish Her, LLC
310 1/2 Main Street South
Stillwater, Minnesota 55082
www.publishherpress.com

Cover design by Kayla Franz

PUBLISH **HER**™

For the four of us.

"And I shall remember you, and a new song as well."

—The Homeric Hymn to Demeter

Contents

Prologue

It is early 2009. I am married to my second husband, Aaron. A man who won't rock the Ferris wheel car because he knows it scares me. A man who materialized in my life just weeks after my divorce was final in 2004, as though fate had him waiting in the wings. A man who still feels, to me, like a prize.

We have been looking at land to buy and build a house on, closer to the city where I work as a psychiatric nurse practitioner. We want to be out of the cookie-cutter condo in suburban Columbus, Ohio. Somewhere, not so much far away, just farther. Preferably somewhere in the country.

On this particular cold and blustery day, we drive an hour to look at a property just far enough away from I-70. Turning off the interstate, we head west on state route 29, through Mechanicsburg, one of Ohio's many anytowns. At a gas station we turn right onto Parkview, cross state route 161, then left onto Long Pond. It's on this road I've never been on that I begin to feel it. A connection, a pull, a familiarity I cannot explain. An uncanny, unbidden sense that I'm coming home. Right onto McAdams then, and there it is, on the left—a wholly unremarkable, drab, long untended field. We pull to the edge of the road, weeds scraping the undercarriage.

The land isn't much to look at—at all—but as I stand in the middle of it with the wind cutting through to my legs despite the long johns under my jeans, that strange, familiar sense becomes stronger. Not deja vu, but a mix of longing and belonging, as though every choice and every circumstance of my life has led me right here to this scrubby patch of land, a place which seems to have been waiting all this time, for me.

We walk in silence. Withered weeds crunch under our boots. The wind rustles through the trees. We wonder how much of the woods is included. About two acres of it, Aaron thinks he remembers the Realtor saying. From the woods on the western edge of the property, the land slopes gently down toward the north.

"The hill's on the wrong side," Aaron says.

For the earth-friendly home we envision building, the house would be nestled in a hill facing south, to take advantage of thermal mass and passive solar gain. The way the land sits now, the house would face north.

"Hills can be moved, can't they?" I ask.

Aaron doesn't reply.

"All we'd need is a bulldozer."

He glances at me, a small smile forming on his lips. "You think it's that easy, don't you?"

I shrug and give him the same small smile. "Isn't that why it's called an earthmover?"

In the weeks to come, we keep looking at land. Too small, too expensive, too close to the interstate. Nothing else we see feels as right to me as the nine-acre parcel with the wrong-facing hill.

"Tell me again why we can't move the hill," I say to Aaron, and we drive out to look one more time.

The Gathering Begins

A little over a year after my father died at age 68 of liver cirrhosis, after my sister and I cleared out his house and divvied up his stuff, I was ready to be free of the past. Or at least to be free enough to start to make sense of it. By this time, my stepmother was already dead, too. As was my mother and all my grandparents.

"We're for real orphans now," my sister and I joked.

It was the autumn of 2016 and I was 44 years old, living in a house that had belonged to my husband Aaron's sister, who had also recently died. Our stay there would be temporary, only until the house we were building in the country was livable. The house we were building ourselves out of tires, bottles, pallet wood and other discarded things. We had been at it for three years already; it might take 10 more. We were patient people, Aaron and I, confident in our abilities. My job as a psychiatric nurse practitioner provided enough money and time to pursue such a project. And also to pursue my real passion, writing, as well as its precursor, pondering.

While I was an inherently happy person, clearing out my father's house had stirred up many emotions. Sadness, for sure. Anger and resentment, too. But mostly a sense of loss and of being lost within my own family. While my sister and I sifted through all the things never meant for us, we found ourselves asking the questions we'd been asking for years: "Do you think Mom and Dad ever loved each other?" "Why do you think she really left him?" "What do you think made her go crazy?" "Do you think either one of them ever wanted us?"

My sister had three kids of her own by this time, and I had all the patients I cared for in my small practice. We both had loving second husbands and we had each other. And even though we both still had questions, it seemed I was the only one who needed answers.

Everything in the house where Aaron and I were living had belonged to my sister-in-law and, as she had many heirlooms from various family members, the house held a rich history. But it wasn't mine. I felt like a transplant—rootless and wanting, in both senses of the word. Deficient and desirous to know from who and where and why I'd come. I was in that time of life where I was no longer young but not yet old. Experienced enough to know that my future happiness depended in large part on my interpretation of the past. I suppose if one believed what my nursing school advisor used to tell me about crisis also meaning opportunity, I was in the throes of a mid-life opportunity. The opportunity to reexamine my life narrative.

And so, I began to write. What came out initially were all the age-worn narratives: my father drank too much; my mother was a crazy living ghost; my stepmother hated us; my sister and I were left alone and on our own. How true were those stories, though? Were they based on facts? Verifiable memories? Or were they just things I'd been telling myself for so long I had come to assume their trueness? How much could I even trust my memories? My memory had been unreliable—a not-so-proverbial cracked sieve. Also, I was prone to hyperbole and melodrama. Surely, what I considered the "real story" must have been colored by these quirks of character.

My old way of seeing things would not do. I needed to look at things with new eyes. I wanted to find the deeper truth of my family's story, of my own story. I wanted to consider all aspects, take all things into account. But how would I go about it? There was a distinct limit to what I could do on my own and, though my sister could act as a guide of sorts through this retelling, all the other players were dead. Even if alive, though, they would have been little help. Silence had been as prevalent in my family as sadness. Where else could I turn?

Around that time, I happened upon a book by Dubravka Ugresic called "The Museum of Unconditional Surrender." In it, she talked about "chance objects," the things that manage to remain in our possession over the years despite our exiles and wanderings. They are the photographs and knickknacks and other things that stay with us in physical form until we are ready to glean their "deeper logic." This made me think of two things:

First, I thought of my father's stained glass workshop and how I had loved the box of shards the most. The uncut glass was lovely but sterile, to be used according to a careful plan with little room for error or spontaneity. But the shards? Why would my father have kept those misfit pieces if they did not hold some potential usefulness? Maybe even some deeper logic? As a child, I'd often wonder what kind of pattern might emerge if one took the time to arrange them just so.

Second, I thought of one of my and my mother's favorite novels, "Of Human Bondage" by W. Somerset Maugham. In it, the protagonist, Philip Carey, mused about the meaning of life by way of a scrap of Persian rug a friend gave to him: "As the weaver elaborated his pattern for no end but the pleasure of his aesthetic sense, so might a man live his life, or if one was forced to believe that his actions were outside his choosing, so might a man look at his life, that it made a pattern."

So might a woman look at her life, I thought. Could I gather up the various shards, my chance objects of the past, to help me find my way to a new pattern, a new story? One that would let me sit back, and finally say, "Yes, that's how it was; that's a story one can move forward from."

However I chose to retell the story, it would have to begin with my parents. I would need to fit those pieces first.

My father's stained glass workshop was always in the basement of whatever house in whatever city he lived. He was an analyst for IBM ("I've been moved," as employees used to say). Over the course of 25 years, he was moved to Cleveland, Columbus, Detroit and back to Cleveland again, with lots of business trips across the country in between. He was an important, albeit generic, man on the go in his crisp white shirts and shined wingtips. He was adept at fitting in. A born corporate man if ever there was one.

He was not as adept at fatherhood. Perhaps he could've been if given the chance. But my mother—a staunch bohemian who could not abide my father's constant social striving or his just as constant drinking—left him when my sister and I were young, the two of us in tow as she set out for Florida, daring to dream of new and better things.

As kids, during our annual visits back to my father's, he'd let my sister and me watch him work. How special those times were to me. My father was most himself in his workshop, and to be in that space with him provided me a sense of maybe not total belonging, but at least a sense of being welcomed.

The workshop reflected his personality—creative yet highly organized. The 12-by-12 sheets of uncut glass were stored upright in a cabinet I wouldn't doubt he designed himself. A large wooden box held the shards. An array of soldering irons lay neatly side by side on the broad workbench, while the various spools of solder sat nearby at the ready. I could recall how the hot iron would hiss, steam rising from the tip, when my father set it on the wet sponge that sat in its own plastic dish. And how my nose would crinkle from the acrid odor of cooling metal.

In an old coffee mug, glass cutters rested, their oiled tips wiped clean on a neatly folded, frayed and faded hand cloth. Also in the mug, breaking pliers, rollers, scissors and nippers. On another bench behind the workbench, there were cigar boxes filled with like things, some labeled in my father's careful all-cap print: COPPER FOIL. STENCILS. PENCILS. PENS. Outside the boxes, larger things were arranged neatly by kind. Protective dust masks and eyewear. The special stand for his pipes. A ceramic ashtray with the name of the casino or resort from where he got it clearly visible on the bottom, the shiny stainless steel multi-tool pipe cleaner balanced in one of the grooves. On a shelf along the wall, empty bottles of Jack Daniels and other remnants of the dismantled bar that used to be in the house he once shared with my mother. Tacked on the wall, a POW/MIA flag from a war he rarely spoke about.

And in the air, the smell of tobacco and cutting oil.

He worked to music. Either smooth jazz on the radio or James Taylor on the tape deck. He also had cassettes of Carly Simon, Frank Sinatra, and Simon and Garfunkel. One of the few things he and my mother shared was a dislike for rock and roll, a rare thing for two people raised in the '50s.

I say worked because my father approached stained glass seriously. He planned each project carefully. Even the small mirrors he'd let us help make during our grade school visits were drawn out first on a piece of large graph paper, each section plotted out and measured (twice) before the soldering iron was even plugged in. And when the soldering of the glass did begin— our job usually being the taping of the cut glass with copper foil to prepare for soldering—his movements were slow, his hands steady, and his brows furrowed behind his glasses as he bent over the table breathing evenly through the filtering cotton of the mask on his face.

If only he had taken such care with us, his first wife and his girls. Maybe my mother wouldn't have left him. Maybe she wouldn't have become mentally ill. Maybe my sister and I would never have felt unwanted and alone. Maybe we could've been one of those families—you know, the happy ones.

Could we have been, though? If certain cares had been taken, could we have dodged unhappiness? Of course not. Other difficulties would have ensued. The choices we make, both deliberate and impulsive, only get us so far. There is always fate to contend with, and suffering is part of everyone's destiny. What matters is what suffering makes of us, what we make of it.

Take glass. Glass is the product of simple sand exposed to tremendous heat—3,090 degrees Fahrenheit, to be exact. Once the sand melts then cools, it does not revert to sand but is transformed into something else entirely, something that defies logic. An amorphous solid, glass exists forever suspended between two seemingly contradictory worlds—the ordered one of the solid, the random of the liquid. Within its apparent strength, an inherent fragility.

"Amorphous" comes from the Greek, "without shape," but glass is able to take shape, and we are able to take glass and make from it what we want. Once, in a History of Ancient Philosophy class at Ohio Wesleyan University, where I was striving to make something—anything—out of myself, I jotted down in a notebook: "Harmony consists of opposing tensions." Had my father thought about this perplexing nature of glass as he made his careful cuts, arranging each piece according to his will? Had he realized the mystery and miracle in his hands?

Unlike my father, who was more a craftsman in my opinion, my mother was an artist. I wish I could have inhabited her creative space as well as I could my father's, but she didn't have just one space, and my memory of her was not as keen.

There was an easel in the living room of our double-wide in the Southwest Florida trailer park where we lived after the divorce. There were various pen and ink drawings of Native Americans in progress. She admired indigenous peoples, perhaps for their views on nature and respect for all living things, but also, I'm sure, because she loved the underdog. There were oil paintings too, hanging above the piano, in the bathroom, her bedroom. All portraits—my mother was not a landscape kind of gal. I imagine she sketched whenever and wherever the mood took hold of her, likely at the kitchen table with a cup of instant coffee and a cigarette within reach.

The year of her breakdown, she had been painting a mural at the Science of Mind Center, where the three of us spent most Sundays. Nowadays it is called the Center for Spiritual Living. It doesn't preach so much as present a synthesis of common truths from all religions, with a focus on our role as co-creators of our lives. The mural scene at the center was a colorful animal collage in the children's room. A panoply of God's creations: lion, lamb, baboon and croc. Antelope, tiger, snake and giraffe. Aardvark, bear cub, elephant, toad. All manner of birds. Some lizards. Some bugs. Predator and prey, all together and getting along. A harmony of opposing tensions. My mother let me paint the bug legs. They were down low where I could reach. Even then my hands shook thanks to a dystonic tremor, and the tiny legs came out squiggly. My mother didn't mind, she was gracious like that. Unlike my father, who insisted on perfection in his art and in his life, my mother could live with messiness.

My mother had musical talent as well, raw and untrained, for which she was both boastful and apologetic. "I never had a lesson," she'd tell us in near the same breath as "I don't know if I can play this one" whenever my friend Heather or I picked out a song from the "Super Hits of the '70s" songbook. Always my mother would say she couldn't play it, and always she could.

"Super Hits of the '70s" was a two-volume set, each book as thick as a Sears catalog. "Tie a Yellow Ribbon," "Love Will Keep Us Together," "Feelings," "Send in the Clowns." Love and loss. Separation and connection. These songs comprised the soundtrack to my childhood.

My mother's hands were strong and confident as they flew over the keys, turquoise rings clattering, a cigarette smoldering in a dirty ashtray on the piano's ledge. Sometimes, she'd hum along or sing off-key in a strained falsetto. As her foot tapped rhythmically, and her hands moved up and down the octaves, her eyes would read the music intently.

And when it was time, she'd nod her head for one of us to turn the page.

In 2016, it was time to turn my own page, to embrace my midlife opportunity and discover a new and truer story, if I could, of my family, of myself. One that might guide me through the next season of my life. Balancing as best I could the careful attention of my father with my mother's willingness to get messy, I began to gather my own chance objects: photographs, my old journals, my father's journals from his 20s, my mother's journals from the last five years of her life, letters, official documents, knickknacks, and my doodles.

I have been a doodler since college. I call them "doodles" because they are born from my subconscious, not my imagination. I don't render them into existence so much as they seem to choose to be expressed. Whenever I try to draw something on purpose, the image is crude and uninspired. But, when I let the pen or pencil or crayon do its thing, what comes out is usually the beginning of something surprising and engaging, which I can then enhance.

One doodle in particular drew me in from the start: a girl gathering apples. She seemed to symbolically reflect the task upon which I was embarking. "Gather," she seemed to say, as I stared at her night after night. "As you are able, so you must."

I Googled "apple symbolism" and found a quote from "Women Who Run with the Wolves" by Clarissa Pinkola Estes. It wasn't a book I had ever read, but the quote was so fitting for what I thought the doodle was trying to tell me: "As with apples, it takes time for maturation, and the roots must find their ground and at least a season must pass, sometimes several."

Several seasons indeed had passed. New roots had found some ground. But I was seeking those that ran deep, the ones formed before my first and second marriage, before this good and surprising life. Even more, I was seeking a mature version of my life thus far, one that would examine all the assumptions and hopefully shed some of the hurts.

I bought the book and read the story of the Handless Maiden, each phase of her adventure as inevitable as it was necessary. Somehow she knew that "to wander is a very good choice." At the end of the ancient tale, the hands of the maiden eventually grew back "through [her] travails and yet [her] good care." For the maiden dwelling in my doodle, my subconscious—my Gathering Girl—it seemed her hands would grow back as she held what she had gathered. What she gathered might be a matter of fate; she was not in control of all that had befallen. But the act of gathering, that was her choice. That was my choice.

Her eyes struck me, too. The left eye, like her left hand, fully formed, her right eye clouded over. She was a portrait of contradiction, caught between opposing tensions, her heavy shoes treading on tender, grabby roots, while seeming bowed down by the lofty weight of hope.

I saw my father and mother in the Gathering Girl doodle. My father with heavy feet, settling, making the best of what was, while my mother—bold girl!—dared to fly. I also saw my mother in those heavy feet, settling in her own way, while my father—bold boy!—dared to follow his ambition. Each one the same, each one a paradox.

And there I was, too, gathering what I could, thinking about the mystery that was my family. The questions unanswered. The questions never asked. The answers I didn't think were true and the ones I wished were not. I thought about how members of a family, their stories so tightly woven together, could be so fragile and estranged. There were many things I wanted to know.

One:

Beginnings

Wholeness

We—my father, my mother, my sister and I—lived in a house in Maple Heights, Ohio, that I remember being blue.

In my memory of this house that may or may not have been blue, it was perpetually 11 o'clock at night. My mother was working at "The Plain Dealer," Cleveland's newspaper. I was sitting on my father's lap, my favorite place, eating Cool Whip out of the container. We were watching the news. Someone had died of frostbite in the downtown area. "The Blob" would be the late night movie.

My father puffed on his pipe and sipped a beer.

I nestled down.

The Cool Whip was light on my finger, but rich on my tongue. It tasted like putting my hand in the flour canister felt. Soft and safe. I ate as much as I wanted. I never got sick.

As I thought about those nights in Maple Heights (which, knowing the fickle nature of memory, may have only been one night or no nights), I tried to conjure the feelings of softness and safeness. Of wholeness.

Once Upon a Tender Time

I had no memory of the four of us, together, as a family. All I had was a photograph my sister obtained after our mother's death. It had been buried among many others in a box my sister carted from Colorado to Alaska to South Dakota and finally to Ohio. Taken at Christmastime 1973, it was a small but epic find. Enduring proof that once upon a tender time we had been a family.

In the photo, we were sitting on my father's parents' hearth in their house in Norwalk, Ohio. A red felt wreath hanging above our heads, made by my Grandma Hoyt, got as much attention as the four of us did in the throwaway. In our current digital age, it's the shot that would've been deleted straight off. Where was the good family Christmas portrait? The one where we were centered and focused, all smiling at the camera, looking like a family should? It was nowhere that I could find. Having dug through all the boxes and emptied all the envelopes, having flipped through all the albums and searched every drawer, I found only three photos of the four of us. And it was that one—that dud dug out of a box my mother kept until her death, that dud my sister saved from the trash heap—that was the only one remotely worthy of mention.

I considered the picture an epic find as though I'd never seen it before. But I was sure I had. As a child, I'd spent hours poring over photos trying to make sense of who my family once was, where I came from. As I revisited the picture, I recognized it as I did all of us in it, as well as the surroundings in which we were posed. Everything was familiar. If I concentrated, I could even conjure the smell of my grandparents' house. The woodsmoke from the fireplace. The sour smell of my grandparents' holiday cocktails. The new fabric smell of those matching Christmas dresses.

And yet, everything seemed strange. Was that woman holding my sister on her lap really the woman who would leave my father with us in tow in just a few years' time? Would she really develop a chronic mental illness and disappear in ways I never imagined possible? Was that man holding me really the man who would, soon after our leaving, marry a woman who would take him from us? Would he really, after this second wife dies, quietly drink himself to death? And those two girls. Were those the girls who would grow to feel they never had either parent? That they were on their own?

The picture left me feeling as bewildered as the expression on my face appeared. I found it hard to believe we were ever a family, despite the proof. I found it equally hard to imagine a time when my parents may have liked each other; they were so different. And yet, there was a sense of intimacy about the way they were positioned in the photo. Perhaps it was only a sense of familiarity I saw. In the same box, I found similar pictures of two of my father's three brothers, each Hoyt boy staged the same— on the hearth, beneath the wreath—with his young wife and children. Although choices would be made in the years to come that would cause all these marriages to fail and the families to scatter like spilled seeds, on that day, at least, everybody knew where and what they were supposed to be.

If the house in Maple Heights had ever been blue, it was no longer. I got the address off my birth certificate, which I kept in an unlocked metal lock box with other important documents (my first marriage license and divorce decree, my mother's autopsy report, my second marriage license) and looked it up online.

The house—a modest Cape Cod under 1,000 square feet built in 1951—was now tan with brown shutters. It still had a front porch, but the steps were to the side, not in the front as I remembered. The tree near the road was still there, but the box hedges running the length of the driveway were gone; what a massive uprooting that must have been.

Studying the house that was my first home, I easily recalled the neighborhood kids, their names full and mythical in my memory. Their images, though, were fuzzy, merely remnants of photographs pored over in the past. But how vividly the feeling of excited fear came back to me, of cool dusks spent with these older children, playing Witch in the Well and Sly Fox.

From the satellite view, I could see the two-car detached garage in the back to the right. I used to ride my bicycle up and down the driveway, the training wheels rattling beneath me. A girl close to my age lived next door, and my mother used to tell a story of how I once ran away with her to get married. The girl had given me a ring, the story went. Made promises. We were discovered along the edge of Interstate 480 just a few blocks to the north. My mother—hysterical with worry, she used to tell me—sent me to my room for the rest of the day. The girl was outside within an hour eating a Popsicle. I thought that was very unfair; the whole thing had been her idea.

In the backyard, the log play cabin my father built for us was long gone. So was the pool he filled on hot summer days. So was whatever may have been my family.

Though I had no memory of us as a family, I did remember something about that time in my young life. Rather, some things:

There was the bedroom I shared with my sister. It was painted bright orange and yellow. I used to peel chips of paint off the wall as I waited for sleep to come.

"Do you think we ate them?" I'd asked my sister.

"I wouldn't doubt it," she had said.

The vivid colors were a stark contrast to what I recall of the rest of the house. The pale blue velour couch, the oak rocker with the wine-colored cushion, the dull wood trim. Even the twin side tables with the whimsical puzzle tops my parents supposedly created together were a dark and muted pattern. The bedroom would've been my mother's doing. My father would never have liked colors that bold.

Other random things: The staircase inside was steep. I had a small wooden chair I liked to sit on. I dressed up as Casper the Friendly Ghost for Halloween. I once cried on my sister's birthday when I didn't get any presents. I had my first dream during those years, of Frankenstein chasing me through dark streets.

Those memories seemed to exist unto themselves, fixed in time and space, singular. Yet, they also seemed to hover together, waiting for me to make of them what I could. At the heart of it all a question: Were we ever a whole and happy family?

Without reliable memories, it was hard to piece together who we were. I tried to glean what I could from the artifacts I gathered, like the throwaway picture, the random memories. I also had my sister to help fill in the gaps, though her memory at times was not much better than mine.

"I remember they fought a lot," my sister had told me. "And I once stabbed Mom."

"I thought you only thought about stabbing her, with a pair of sewing scissors."

For this conversation, we were in our 40s, driving together to visit our mother's remaining family in rural Ohio. My sister insisted we keep in touch with our relatives. "Family's important," she always told me. "And these people actually like us."

About the stabbing, my sister set me straight. "I really did stab her. With a giant-ass needle."

We both laughed in a way that may have seemed inappropriate to outsiders. But we were insiders, and laughter was the way we always kept it together.

"We were living in Maple Heights, right?" I asked her. I had heard the story before but apparently didn't remember it correctly.

She nodded. "I was probably in first grade. I don't know. I wasn't even mad. I just did it."

"That's so awful," I said. "What'd Mom do?"

"Well, she wasn't very happy."

By all accounts, I was the happiest in our family of four. My father once told me he loved coming in to wake me up in the mornings because I'd just sit up and smile.

"You were such a happy baby," I remembered him telling me, though I couldn't recall where or when. But I could see him sitting on the edge of a chair, puffing on his pipe, the smell rich and sweet and familiar, smiling a smile I wish I had seen more often—open and unselfconscious—his shoulders hunched slightly from a few too many beers or glasses of wine. He would only talk about the past when he was drinking. Sober, he was reserved, reticent, uptight even, careful of what he said and who he said it to. He was a company man who held fast the company line. After many drinks he'd get looser.

"I remember when you were born," he told me that time or another, one manicured hand cupping the other that cradled his pipe. He was a solidly handsome man with soft blue eyes and a jawline not quite square enough to hide a boyish vulnerability. "I was afraid you two wouldn't make it," he said, hanging his head and giving it a small shake. This was my father opening up. He said he listened to James Taylor's "Fire and Rain" over and over, hoping we'd be OK. He didn't look at me as he spoke, and when he was done, he brought the pipe to his thin lips and our moment vanished.

"You were early," my mother once told me. "Like you couldn't wait to get here."

As with my father, I could picture her telling me this, though again I couldn't place the when or where. No matter, she would have been sitting at the kitchen table, a glass of iced tea or cup of black instant coffee in front of her, cigarette in hand. With her other hand she would have fingered the mole on the lower right side of her face. She wasn't pretty so much as attractive, with deep hazel eyes and cheekbones made for smiling. She had a physical sturdiness that belied an emotional fragility.

I arrived in the world at the end of April 1972, on my mother's birthday, which always made me feel special. My mother had lost two or three babies between my sister and me, depending on the version of the story. The doctor told my mother to abort me; I'd never make it to term. Later in life, she would write about it in her journal, using my childhood nickname: "Amy's my love child. My doctor said mother and child wouldn't make it." But I did. Maybe that's why I was so happy.

I asked my sister what she remembered about me being born and what kind of baby I was.

"I don't really remember," she told me. "But everybody loved you."

My father was in Vietnam in the winter of early 1969 when my sister was born. She had been conceived the previous spring, a few months before my parents married and he shipped out. As my mother had always told the story, when she met my father at the airport upon his return home—new baby in her young arms—my father was drunk and said, "How do I know that's mine?" He was likely only making a crude soldier's joke, but still. It was one of many slights my mother would carry for the rest of her life. And my sister, I ached when I thought of what she once told me about her presence in the world: "I am the living reminder of their greatest mistake."

I've often imagined that moment my mother recounted. I have pictured the three of them posed as in a snapshot, frozen in time. My mother wearing something second-hand and denim with a kerchief tied around her hair, holding my infant sister insecurely in her arms. My father with his Air Force duffel slung over his shoulder, wearing his favorite suit and carefully shined shoes. He would've brushed his hair right before deboarding. My mother would have just crushed out a cigarette. They had been separated for over a year. Did they embrace? Exchange a kiss? My mother would've been so angry—had been so angry—about his drunkenness, his casual cruelty. And my father would've been annoyed with my mother's smoking and her cheap clothes.

To be fair, this was my mother's version. But my father's story of his homecoming corroborated part of hers: "The first thing I did when I left 'Nam was get drunk."

Despite my sister's possible unwelcomed entrance into the world, she held pleasant memories of our parents in those early years. She told me that our mother made us clothes and baked cookies and painted flowers on old furniture. She told me our father built us the log play cabin in the backyard and filled the above-ground pool with cold hose water on hot summer days.

I vaguely remembered the baking, putting my hand in the flour canister, that indelible feeling of wholeness, though I could not place my mother there. I vividly remembered the pool. I could see my father holding the hose. Could smell the plastic, warmed by the sun. Could feel the water as I slipped in, shocking but pleasant. My father was in the pool with me, wading waist high, his arms reaching out for me as I dog-paddled toward him. This could have been a fabrication. Some of it, anyway. The sensory memories were accurate—at least strong and easy to conjure. And somewhere I'd seen a picture of my father and me in the pool. I wanted to believe in moments like this. So, I did.

Yet, no matter how much I tried, I couldn't seem to create any such memories of my mother.

I listened to my sister when she shared what she remembered about our family and felt reassured at the picture of normalcy her memories painted. But I also felt the picture wasn't complete.

"But what were we like as a family?" I asked her. "The four of us?"

Always, a shrug. "We all kind of did our own thing."

Disconnection. It was my strongest emotional memory when I thought of the four of us. Other than the memories I held closely of my father and me, I had an overarching sense of being separate from my parents, especially from my mother. I didn't remember being tucked in at night, read a bedtime story, rocked to sleep. Neither did my sister.

But just when I thought I'd fit the memories into their proper places, I'd experience a moment like this: I was watching a show with Aaron about a serial killer who kills serial killers. The main character, the titular killer, was singing "Brother John" to his girlfriend's children as he tucked them in. A memory came flooding back of my mother singing the same song to us, in English and in French. More of a knowing than a memory. I recalled the words: "Frère Jacques, Frère Jacques, dormez-vous? Dormez-vous?" I imagined the little girl I was then, enthusiastic and unselfconscious, belting out the words. "Ding, dang, dong! Ding, dang, dong!"

"My mother used to sing us that song, I think," I told Aaron, lingering on the sweet, sad mix of longing and belonging the song evoked, a song that I had, up to that moment, forgotten.

Still, the memories of disconnection loomed.

Like one where I was up early one morning, alone. I poured myself a bowl of Cheerios, dumped several spoonfuls of sugar on top, and opened the refrigerator only to find there was no milk. Instead of getting my mother or my father, or even my sister, I mixed water and sugar into a cup, thinking the white sugar with the water would make milk. It did not. I abandoned it and ate my Cheerios in front of the television, pleasantly surprised when I found all the sugar in the bottom of the bowl. I ate it, one wet fingerful at a time, and thought, "I should always eat my Cheerios like this."

The memory could have been false. It had a quality I didn't quite trust, fitting too perfectly the belief I had about myself: I did OK on my own, I didn't need anyone. Was that memory a true reflection of who I was then, or was I reconstructing it to align with who I had become? Who I was becoming? Was the trait of self-reliance something I developed early on to withstand the disconnection I believed defined the four of us? Was my memory of disconnection even accurate?

Another memory, more believable to me and verified by my sister, of a night around Christmas. My sister and I were in our room singing "Jingle bells, Batman smells …" at the top of our lungs. We were shouting out the last line about Joker getting away when the door flew open and my father screamed at us to shut our damn mouths. My mother, I imagined, was behind him, possibly crying. They were fighting and we were interrupting. It was the closest I could get to a memory of them together at that time, but even then they were off camera, peripheral.

They were not with my sister and me when we propped the long coffee table up on the couch in the basement to make a slide. They were not with us out front under the tree when we played with the neighborhood kids. They were not with us when we tucked ourselves in a sleeping bag and slid down the steep attic stairs.

They were not with us. But they were there. We were all there, once.

Recollections of disconnection and of possible aloofness aside, there was ample evidence that our parents were loving and attentive. There were, for instance, many professional portraits of us as children. Perhaps dressing us up and posing us this way and that was only for show, but still, it would have taken time. It would've taken effort. And there was at least one candid shot I found of a Christmas morning, the living room strewn with wrapping paper, the tree decorated, and four stockings labeled and hung with care. My sister was sitting on her ankles, staring at the camera, making a funny face. She was holding her new toy, the owl-shaped Novus Quiz Kid calculator. I was standing rigid in excitement, my expression ecstatic as I held up the new stuffed dog I received. And my mother. She was behind me sitting in the rocker with the wine-colored cushion that my sister and I took out of our father's house after he died. My mother was leaning forward and smiling broadly at my sister. Her whole face aglow. I wished I could remember my mother then, that way. My father, no doubt, was the one taking the picture. Indirect proof of another time we were together, as a family.

There was also our annual family vacation to Myrtle Beach. "I always burned," my sister had told me. "And our babysitter used to go with us." My mother, later in life, would tease me about how much I loved prancing around in my bathing suit. She'd sing in her off-key voice about my "itsy-bitsy teenie-weenie yellow polka-dot bikini," snapping her fingers and swiveling her hips unrhythmically in a way that always made me laugh. But in my mind, she was nowhere on the beach with me. Nor was my sunburned sister. My father wasn't even there. Only some boy my age named Joey. My plastic pail and shovel. The sand. The sun.

My father rarely spoke about the trips to South Carolina other than to comment occasionally that he never understood why my mother left him. "I gave her everything." To him, those yearly vacations were part of the everything he had given, including the nice house, the pool, the gift-filled Christmas mornings. All trappings of a normal, happy family. On the surface at least, all was well, complete, as it should be.

While alive, my parents were no help. Neither of them ever told stories about the four of us. Sometimes they spoke of each other. My mother would tell me stories about times my father got drunk and embarrassed her in front of his company friends. My father would tell stories about how my mother would get angry because he would go to the store to buy beer and purposefully forget her cigarettes. There were never stories about how they met, how they fell in love (if they fell in love). My mother freely shared recollections of my sister and me. Favorite stories, of my sister getting hoof-and-mouth disease from playing in graveyard dirt, of me insisting on wearing a bathing cap during toilet training. I remembered her laughing, all of us laughing, as my sister and I pieced these proffered memories into a mental picture we could keep with us and look at later—our childhood.

My father, for his part, shared what he could, but he had little patience for piecemeal reminiscing. Aside from the few stories that would spill out after a few too many drinks, he held on to just one view of that tender time: We were once everything a family was supposed to be. It seemed he alone carried that image of us.

I went back to the actual image of the four of us, the photograph, and tried to glean what I could about who our family was, how things were between us. Were we, as my father apparently believed, a whole and happy family? Or were we merely four beings thrown into a story, never fully completing the picture of what we were expected to be?

It was hard to tell. I resorted to tools.

At a glance it looked like my mother was smiling tenderly at my sister; but on closer inspection with flashlight and magnifying glass, I saw my mother wasn't smiling at all.

Her expression took me aback. I peered closer. She looked thoughtful, sad maybe. "This isn't where we're supposed to be," she could have been whispering to my sister, foretelling things to come. But I saw something else, too. Though there had never been any evidence that my mother showed signs of mental illness before she left my father, her expression in the image was so like the flat, stony affect that would haunt me after her mental breakdown. Was I only seeing it because I knew what happened? Possibly. Maybe she was simply caught off guard when the picture was snapped. Maybe everything was just fine. Maybe we were a whole and happy family.

My sister's smile, distinct in the dim photograph even without the aid of tools, spoke to this. But her smile had been suspect, even at that young age. "I don't think I've ever been happy," my sister used to tell me, her sad refrain for many years. But she had always been adept at that brave face, which is why I didn't always trust her smile.

My father, looking handsome despite his front-heavy hairdo and pointed shirt collar, seemed to be smiling mischievously straight at the camera. He was either drunk or planning to get drunk as soon as he could. His parents, drinkers themselves, would have already mixed him one of their Christmas cocktails.

On second look, though, it appeared my father might not have been smiling either.

Perhaps it was resignation I saw. My father believed in making the best of things. And though this family wasn't part of the adventure he meant to choose for himself, he wasn't the type of man to walk away.

I looked at my own image. That little girl seemed to be thinking the same thing I thought years later: What am I to make of it all? How do all these pieces fit? What picture emerges?

We were together, certainly, at least on the surface of things. But was there anything deeper between us? Did we ever have that bond, that connection, I assumed other families felt? I couldn't see it. No matter how I rearranged the bits I'd gathered so far, we seemed to remain separate, thrown together, our shared roots shallow, stunted and estranged. How did one grow from such soil? How did one thrive?

Dear Tom; Dear Susan

P erhaps I needed to look back further. Before I was born. Before my sister was born.

Jul. 12, 1968, to be exact.

A girl, 20 years old and eight weeks pregnant, married a boy who would never be madly in love with her. The boy was just a little older, 21, and would go to Vietnam in a month. Unlike most of his peers, he was choosing to go to war.

The girl's mother was stern—a Cold Prickly, you might say (the opposite of the Warm Fuzzy I used to get in grade school when I did something good). The mother insisted the girl wear a mid-length dress, having lost her right to a fairy-tale wedding when she let the boy who would never be madly in love with her take her out for pie.

That piece of pie would cost the girl; she would have no fancy bouquet on her big day, let alone a Warm Fuzzy.

I tried to imagine what they both must have felt on their wedding day, that girl and that boy, my parents. Was the girl's wig—worn to hide her curly, unruly hair—itchy at her hairline? Was the boy's suit not yet a second skin? Did they each feel their imagined futures disappearing as they said their scripted lines?

My mother, story went, had a full scholarship to an art school. She was a talented gal with pen, pencil, any kind of paint. She had potential. She had promise. She hadn't meant to have a baby.

My father, story went, had another girl—Callie Smith—an iconic figure in my family mythology, forever referred to by her full name. On my father's list of addresses in one of his journals, Callie Smith was number five. My mother, known then simply as Sue Debolt, was number four. I didn't know how my father met Callie Smith, or where, or whether my mother knew what she meant to my father, but she was neck and neck with my mother for my father's attention as early as '66.

"This is the woman who should have been your mother," my father said to me one night when I was at his house, on break from college. I was 20. We were in his basement workshop, and his latest project—The monk? The pheasant?—was likely laid out carefully on the table, waiting to be soldered. My father held up an 8-by-10 of a pretty girl with a pretty smile. He was tipsy and misty eyed, signs I would come to learn meant an inappropriate confession was coming. It was the first secret he ever disclosed, though he might say bestowed to me, for he shared the news of Callie Smith as though it were a gift. To me it was a burden. I had always suspected he never loved my mother, and now he was confirming that sad truth.

"I don't think it works that way," was all I could think to say.

I had heard of Callie Smith before, through the family grapevine. Grapevine being the perfect word, as I could not if I tried trace the story back to one source—it seemed to come from everywhere and nowhere, tangled like the tendrils of a vine. The story had my father being in love with Callie Smith when he got my mother pregnant. Always one to do the right thing even when it was wrong, he decided to marry my mother. Fortunately for him, a war was going on. The story had him volunteering for Vietnam and having his friends tell Callie Smith he died overseas, thus avoiding the inconvenience of at least one sad truth. It seemed to me such a cowardly thing to do. It made me not trust him.

My father didn't elaborate on the night of his confession. I was glad he didn't. In one sentence he validated everything I never wanted to believe: My mother wasn't the one he really loved, and he regretted his marriage to her. And by extension, in my young mind, that meant he regretted having had my sister and me. Every happy memory I had ever had of him and me, or of what our family might have been, was shattered in that moment. I felt unloved and angry. Unwanted and resentful. At no time at age 20 did I feel sad. But as I looked back at more than twice of 20, I did. I felt sad for that girl and that boy, even for that other girl. I felt sad for their sad story. And I wanted to know, was it ever a love story?

From my father's journal, 1968:

DATE	IN	OUT	BAL	EXPENDITURE
July 12, 1968	shows me	"Us"	love	Happiness

The column headings were written in my father's all-cap print. The entry—incredibly, to me—was written in my mother's hand, a confident cursive complete with cheerful circle above the "i" in "Happiness." In the four journals I had of my father's, it was a lone entry on the last balance sheet he would keep in those pages.

The entry spoke to my mother's optimism, an unwarranted optimism it seemed to me. After my father's death in 2015, my sister and I found my mother's high school picture in a box my father kept squirreled away. On the back of the picture was a note from my mother to my father: "Tom, to quote you: 'to the boy (girl it was on your picture to me) I'll never be madly in love with.'" Later, I went looking for that high school photo of my father, the one my mother noted. I found it glued to a page in the heavy faux leather photo album I inherited titled "Our Family."

It didn't budge with my gentle prying. I would have to take my mother's word about the message he wrote on the back. That, or get a steamer.

I had no doubt my mother was madly in love with my father. The rest of her high school photo message more than hinted at it: "I owe you so much," she wrote in small, careful print. "I'd like to give you a present, but I can't find a box big enough to put it in or a bow pretty enough to tie around it. I like being with you and I'm proud, yes proud, to be seen with you … If you want that present see me before you leave on the 20th. I'm going to miss you so very, very much. One of your better pals I hope, Sue."

All this to a boy who said he'd never be madly in love with her. I couldn't blame her. When I was young, I wouldn't have been able to resist the coy subtext of such a dramatic pronouncement either. Especially coming from the boy my father had been, with his wavy blonde hair and mischievous blue eyes. His good looks, coupled with his insouciance, surely must have made my mother swoon.

At least in the beginning. Before the war had its way with my father and sent him back a broken but determined version of himself, fueled by drink and a drive to pursue a "first class" life. Before my sister and the two miscarriages. Before the stillborn. Before me. Before my mother realized she wanted more of what my father didn't have to give and started dreaming up a new version of herself. Before she left him, with my sister and me, headed for a new adventure in Florida, where her Cold Prickly mother and father lived. Before all that, I imagined, she loved him.

In 2013, long after my mother was dead and soon after my stepmother died, I sat at my father's house on the patio with him while he drank and I scolded and he said "Just one more" and kept on drinking. His grief at losing his second wife of 30-some years was making him very, very thirsty. During those three decades, and especially during the last few months of her life, his wife had been committed to keeping my father to herself. It was the first chance I had had to really talk to him in years. And he was drunk. I took advantage of it to pry from him another confession.

"Why'd you marry Mom?" I asked. If there was anything to the story of him embracing a war to escape a moment of bad judgment, anything to the story of him breaking the heart of the girl he loved only to have his own heart broken by the one he didn't, I wanted to know.

He puffed on his pipe, shook his head and smiled like the little boy he still was despite the graying hair hiding beneath the blonde dye. "Well, it was between her and Callie Smith, and your mother got pregnant first."

"Wow," was all I could think to say. I tried to identify the emotion his statement provoked in me, and while I did, my father, on this night, elaborated.

Callie was at school in Ann Arbor, Michigan, he told me, while he was stationed in South Carolina. "Your mother took a bus down to visit me. We went out for pie. The next thing I knew, she was pregnant."

I couldn't help but laugh. "It doesn't work that way," I told him, at once amused and annoyed by his ignorance, angry at the idea it might be flippancy.

He laughed too, then his eyes welled up and a look of genuine sorrow crossed his face. "I never understood why she left. I gave her everything. I loved her so much."

He began to sob, the big insatiable waves of grief washing over him. I stood behind him with my arms draped around his shaking shoulders and softly kissed his head, not fully believing him, but wanting to.

I still wanted to believe he loved her once. I turned to what I hoped would yield hard evidence: his journals. My sister and I found them buried in the bottom desk drawer in his den when we cleaned out his house. How they survived my stepmother's prying eyes and her instinct to destroy anything that came before her, I'd never know. But there they were, carefully concealed beneath less momentous things.

My father titled three of the four journals "Record II," "Record III" and "Record IV." At first, I thought him calling his journals records was pretentious, like the way he added an "h" to the shortened version of his name, switching from Tom to Thom, to seem more sophisticated. But when I reached for the first journal for the 50th time to search its pages more closely, I noticed that the small book had the word "Record" embossed in gold on the leathered black cover as well as on the red cloth spine.

All four books were roughly 5-by-8 inches. Large enough to write in comfortably but small enough to carry easily in your hand, or in your coat pocket, or in your Air Force fatigues. The first record was a black and red Wilson Jones lined notebook. The second and third had homemade white jackets taped over drab green hard cloth. Each was labeled in my father's careful print and signed on the bottom right: Thom A. Hoyt. The last one had no homemade cover, no signature, no embossing, simply an "IV" scrawled haphazardly in red pen across the top. Inside was my father's signature in red and the words "Viet Nam 68-69." It was the only one my mother hadn't written in.

Record was a good word for my father's journals. Better, really, than journal. Journal implied more a diary, personal thoughts, at the least a chronicle of one's daily life. My father was more of a recorder. During the short span these four records covered (1966 to 1969), he kept detailed notes of items bought and monies received, books he planned to read, and the cost of going home for a weekend (right down to the $4.40 in toll fees between South Carolina and Ohio).

Most pages, though, were filled with phrases and whole passages from things he read. It appeared he was an avid reader in his early 20s, a young man eager to know the world. He belonged to several book clubs, and appeared to subscribe to "Playboy," "Life" and "Newsweek." Many of the passages he copied were uncredited, leaving me the painstaking task of running most of what he left behind through a plagiarism website to try to find the sources. Little of what he wrote was uniquely his, and little was about love. Even less was about my mother.

The strongest piece of evidence I found was in "Record III." In April and May of '68, before they were married, before he left for the war, there had been this exchange:

Dear Tom,
I love you!
Sue

April 27, 1968

Dear Susan
I will always love you
Tom

16 may 68

To me, those six lines didn't offer proof of his love for her (or hers for him, though they both stated it clearly enough) so much as they illustrated the incongruity between my parents. Maybe that was just because I knew the outcome. I noticed my mother's innocent omission of the "h" in my father's name, her artless use of the present tense, the sincere excitement of that exclamation point. I looked at the way she wrote the date— practical, no airs—and the diminutive way she signed her name.

I compared it to my father's formal "Dear Susan" and his use of the simple future. What simple? What future? So many ways to interpret those five words, left open-ended, unpunctuated. I will always love you though I really love another. I will always love you though never madly. I will always love you though you will one day leave. The way he wrote the date was so worldly, so refined.

And that "h" in Thom!

He was all about appearance, my father. That never changed. His second wife cared more for appearance than he did, and he would stay with her for more than 30 years, out of duty, fear or love—probably all three—until she died suddenly and left him a husk of his former self. My mother, meanwhile, after many missteps and downturns, would find a Tom who was not afraid to exclaim his love for her, simply and unambiguously. My second stepfather, Tom Mayle, used to smile broadly at my mother and yell out "I love this woman!" for all the world to hear.

There was more evidence, of sorts, that my father may have once loved my mother. On the same page as the previous six lines mentioned, my father wrote a spiel comparing her to the most beautiful picture he'd ever seen, the most wonderful symphony he'd ever heard, the fragrance of the exquisite perfume of the Rue de la Paix. Et cetera. To which my mother, while my father was in Vietnam, later responded: "Darling, this is the loneliest time of my life. A year without you is like being half alive. I shall love you terribly when you come home to me finally. I shall deign to prove this to you for the rest of my living years."

I couldn't imagine my mother would have ever suspected my father lifted his words of pictures and symphonies and perfumes from a description of Hungarian Tokay wine found in the pages of a 1967 issue of "Playboy." I only knew this because I found the identical spiel copied in "Record I" and credited appropriately to said magazine.

So my father may have been a plagiarist. I had suspected as much. His records were full of uncredited passages, including a poem he "wrote" for my mother in June of 1968: Ogden Nash's "Always Marry an April Girl." Did he do it for love? He did it a lot. I knew that for a fact.

Yet, when I was about to write my father off as the cad I always believed him to be, I found this in "Record IV" from September of '68, a month after he arrived in Vietnam:

26 Sept 68

The Sea is deep blue,
My emotions are too.
The Waves are frosty white,
As they rush the sandy shore,
As if they were shoved.
How I long for your Kiss tonight,
And miss your precious love,
Susan I will love you for evermore.

51

The poem was unique according to the three plagiarism websites I consulted. He could have stolen it from a fellow homesick staff sergeant, but it still seemed sincere. And the smiley face. That was my father's signature smiley face. The same one that decorated my birthday, Easter and Christmas cards throughout my childhood. A face so familiar, not quite smiling but looking like it wanted to. Even if my father didn't love my mother, I think he wanted to. It would have been the right thing to feel.

More compelling to me in the records was the indirect evidence of my parents' love for each other. Take for instance the fact that my mother wrote in every one of my father's records except the one he took to Vietnam. I could almost imagine my mother taking it upon herself to intrude on his privacy, forcing intimacy that didn't exist. And yet, starting with "Record II," my father kept multiple pages blank between his entries, almost as though he were encouraging my mother to fill in the gaps. She never did, completely. Not even close. There's only one full page of her writing in "Record II," written while he was in Vietnam, a lament about how much she missed him.

Her other contributions in his records were brief. There were comments on the books he listed (she gave Ayn Rand's "Anthem" and "The Fountainhead" both "excellent"). There were gin rummy score sheets of card games played together. And there were random confessions, including one in response to a quote my father copied from Kurt Vonnegut's "Cat's Cradle": "Live by the foma that makes you brave and kind and healthy and happy." To which my mother responded: "Confession: Oct. '68. This is what I did. I embroidered truths."

My father would have been in Vietnam by October 1968, avoiding combat in Cam Ranh Bay with the 485th unit of the Ground Electronics Engineering Installation Agency, as far as I was able to gather, drinking beer and eating steak, according to the account of Tom Vietch, his oldest and closest friend (who I refer to from here on out simply as Vietch, as there are already too many Toms in this story). My mother, meanwhile, would have been in Ohio, anticipating the birth of her first child.

Vonnegut defines "foma" as "harmless untruths." Is this what my mother meant by embroidered truths? Had she embroidered my father's sense of duty to make it appear more like love? Had my father, in his way, done the same? Perhaps their saying "I love you" in these small ways was their shared harmless untruth.

It may sound as though I blamed my father for my parents' sad story. I did, in some ways. I blamed him for taking advantage of a young girl just because he could. I blamed him for abandoning his pregnant wife and possibly concocting a devastating lie to a girl whom he supposedly loved. I blamed him for telling the truth only when he was drunk, when it was hard enough to trust him.

I didn't blame him for my mother leaving and taking us away. I didn't blame her either. It was for the best. Of this one thing, I was (I think) absolutely certain.

And yet, there were things I never considered. What hold might she have had on him? The playful way she spoke about a gift but not having a big enough box. "If you want that present, see me before you leave." The woman I knew was bawdy and hypersexual. She'd told me more than once that the first time her third husband, Tom Mayle, touched her arm, she had an orgasm. I had always thought of my mother's younger self as shy and awkward, with her frizzy hair and broad nose, perhaps projecting onto her my impression of myself at that age. But I began to wonder, was my father drawn to her sexuality? Was she as bold and ribald then as when I knew her as an adult?

Vietch, who knew both my parents in high school, got dreamy-eyed every time he spoke about my mother. "Ah! Your mother … what a knockout." And my father's youngest brother—who was, like all the Hoyt boys, not one for talking— once looked at me and said out of the blue, "You remind me so much of your mother," and teared up. So maybe she wasn't the homely, naive girl I've imagined all those years. Maybe she knew what she was doing, catching this sweet, handsome boy with all his sweet pretensions. Maybe that piece of pie was her idea all along.

Not to mention, there was a war going on. My father would likely have been drafted even if he hadn't enlisted, and by enlisting he managed to avoid combat, serving instead with the

Ground Electronics Engineering Installation Agency, a safer corner of the war as far as my research suggested.

And Callie Smith? She did exist. But whether she received the devastating news of my father's invented death or the news of him marrying another girl, I didn't know. I doubted I ever would.

When my sister and I dug through my father's things after his death in 2015, we found that 8-by-10 of Callie Smith in a box. I held the photo up to the light, marveling at the relic I thought maybe I had made up. I told my sister the story our father had told me about how Callie should have been our mother. We were both silent then, each contemplating the many facets of our parents' story.

"Well, she wasn't our mother," I said, and threw the photo in the trash.

On Jul. 12, 1968, their wedding day, they weren't my mother and father yet. They were just two kids, Tom and Susan, with another kid hidden deep. The photo, a sepia-toned 8-by-10 from "Our Family" album, was overexposed in areas, which gave them a dream-like appearance. My father's shirt collar and boutonniere, his hands, and the arm flanking my mother's side, all looked a little blurry. As did my mother's feet and upper body. They were two people who looked like something wished for but not quite achieved.

My father was unbelievably handsome to me. The kind of handsome that could make a young girl's heart ache for its attention. The kind reminiscent of Steve McQueen or that actor who played the father on "The Brady Bunch." In the photo, my father's square jaw appeared clenched, his close-lipped smile, almost a grimace. He stared straight ahead, but not directly at the camera. What future was he seeing the moment the shutter closed? His hands were clasped in front of him in a funereal manner, but his feet, from my perspective, were placed jauntily perpendicular to one another in a way that reminded me of Frank Sinatra. My favorite detail was the way his head tilted toward my mother.

Meanwhile, my mother—So young! So hopeful looking! So proud?—was all smiles in her white bridal dress, which was indeed, per my Cold Prickly grandmother's insistence, just below the knee. My mother did have a bouquet, despite what I had remembered. The flowers were white like her dress, and the only way I knew they were there was because the green leaves poked out the bottom and her hands were hidden. Her image, more than my father's even, seemed to seep into the background, her right elbow looking especially drippy. Her stance wasn't as confident as my father's, but with her left hand likely holding on to his right arm beneath the invisible bouquet, she seemed to gather enough courage to pivot her right foot daintily away from her left. Her head, donned with both short wig and veil, was turned toward my father, both eyes on him, trusting and loving, even happy.

More than anything else in their wedding photo, their feet told a story. Their left feet faced forward, correct, in line with expectations; but their right feet were out of line, my mother's with that dainty but defiant pivot. "We know what's expected," their feet seemed to say, "but we both want something more." Whose fault that more would turn out to be something else for each of them? Whose fault that their harmless untruth could not sustain them?

I tried not to judge my parents' choices. Tried simply to gather the pieces, to stay open to the patterns revealed. But their choices had consequences, a not-so-simple fact. Their choices led to my sister. To me. Our lives depended on, extended from, theirs. If I never knew the truth about them, could I ever know it about myself?

As for me, I never did get a steamer to verify my mother's story about what my father wrote. "To the girl I'll never be madly in love with." Turned out, I didn't have to. The actual wallet-sized copy of my father's high school photo that he gave my mother was not in "Our Family" album after all. It was in an album I had put together myself, years ago, when I was young. The message he wrote her was indeed on the back, but someone—My mother? My sister? Me?—scratched over my father's original words with a blue pen.

I Googled "how to remove ink from paper" and ended up following, messily, some questionable instructions that involved soaking the photo in vegetable oil. At first, I didn't think it worked. The message appeared even more obscured than before. But later—nearly a year later—when I returned to the photo again, part of a slightly different version of the message peeked through the lines: "I'm not ma … love with …" The only other word I could make out was "still."

Promise, Broken

Whether my mother and father once loved each other, whether we were ever a happy family—still, my mother left.

It was an early morning in late 1976. I was 4; my sister, 7. My mother rustled us out of bed and into the family station wagon. "We're going on a trip," was what my sister remembered her saying. I could imagine my young self bouncing awake that morning, pouncing on my sister, just as easily as I could picture her hiding her head under the pillow and groaning. I tried to imagine my mother. Was she hurried and crying as she packed our things? Or dry-eyed and calm?

I didn't need to imagine the yellow family station wagon. It was as clear to me now as it was then. The interior was a black basket-weave vinyl with a distinct smell. I could almost smell it, sharp and artificial. That time of year, the seat would have been cool to the touch, slippery around turns.

The car was in a photo taken in late 1975 or early 1976, many, many mornings before the morning in question:

It must have been my father standing in the middle of that sandy patch of grass who took the picture. I stared at it for a long while, prodded by a hunch that the apparent throwaway held some deeper truth.

Nothing much was surprising in the picture: my mother's ubiquitous cigarette in her left hand; my sister's annoyed stance; my precious posing. Then it hit me—the composition. The three of us and our family wagon were not quite in the center of the frame. Nor were we balanced with the shadow that the sun cast. We were balanced instead with a lone pole in the background to our right. With the aid of a ruler, I discovered that the car and the pole taken together were almost perfectly centered in the frame, off by a mere 16th of an inch.

Couldn't my father have zoomed in? Stepped closer before snapping the shot?

It was the pole I was hung up on. It stood starkly, stoically alone, just as I imagined my father stood on our front porch months later as he watched his family drive off into the sunrise. The pole's faint wires a symbol for the fragile lines that would connect us in the years to come.

To me, the photograph was premonitory. Presentient. Big moments call for big words, and the moment that the picture portended was a big moment in my family's story. I couldn't help think that my father managed to capture, in some undisclosed part of South Carolina, the intersection of destiny and decision. The picture seemed to already tell the story of my mother leaving.

The picture told another story, the more I looked at it. And only, I was sure, because I knew the history and the outcome. In the photo, I was literally the closest to my father, posing preciously in front of my mother and my sister, who occupied a shared plane. Our positioning was symbolic of our family dynamic. My mother and my sister in one dimension; my father and I, another. I had no doubt that if he had had a choice, he would have chosen me. But he didn't have a choice, as far as I knew. My mother wanted both of us—her girls. Even then, my sister and I were considered a pair, inseparable. Samantha and Amanda. Sami and Amy. We were our mother's children.

But to my 4-year-old self, my father was my world, or so it seemed to me across the span of decades. And everything I had ever known of my world felt right and safe and whole, even if it wasn't, up until the moment my mother left.

"The moment" implies my mother's mind was made in an instant. Maybe it was. I have experienced similar moments of clarity. Moments when the knowledge of the thing I must do was so strong and sure I could almost mistake the feeling for fate—I must choose this. It's as though life tumbles us every which way, down that path, around that bend, until we land at a time and place where we are asked to make a decision. Like those "Choose Your Own Adventure" books I read as a kid. The story went only so far before asking the reader to make a choice, and in making that choice the reader was launched into a new narrative, one solely dependent on the choice made. The choice was an act of free will, but the outcome of that choice was determined. It seems what we take for a dichotomy is not so clear-cut, but rather a nuanced, harmonious dance of opposing tensions. After all, the choices we're asked to make in life are rarely as simple as this or that.

In the early 2000s, at least a year after my mother died, my father and I traveled together from Ohio to visit my sister, who was living in Alaska. We went on the same flight, though he flew first class while I flew coach. I was going on his dime, so I didn't complain. I was more comfortable among my fellow commoners anyway. I hadn't even liked it when the limo driver who took us to the airport insisted on handling my bags. Couldn't my father have just called a taxi?

During our layover, we went to the premier lounge. He ordered a glass of red wine or a bottled import. I got a Diet Coke. This trip to visit my sister was part of the great reconciliation between my father and me. A few years before my mother's death, my first husband and I had gone bankrupt after a venture into real estate investment, and to try to dig out of debt, I had started working at a strip club. I had warned my father that I wouldn't be able to pay on the student loan that was in his name, kept him abreast of everything going on, even let him know I was dancing to assure him I'd be in the black again soon.

I'd realize later how naive I was to expect him not to be upset. His little girl was taking off her clothes for strange men and working with people who used words like "titties" and "conversate." To me, it was just another adventure in a long line of adventures, and a practical one at that. I needed money. Still, his reaction seemed excessive and hypocritical, and it angered me. He had called me morally defective in so many words, accused me of being on drugs. I disowned him for two years and kept a photograph of him posing in a sweatshirt from his favorite nudie bar in Canada to keep the anger fresh.

My mother's unexpected death in the spring of 2000 had brought us back together. I was touched by his concern, impressed that he would know her passing would be difficult for me. I even let it slide when he made a comment about what her life could have been, ignoring the unspoken "If she had stayed with me …"

In the premier lounge, my father and I sipped our drinks. He was still so handsome. I loved the way he smelled, that rich mix of pipe tobacco and aftershave. He looked relaxed to me, which I didn't often see. He was even wearing jeans instead of his normal business suit or casual khakis. Still, his jeans were pressed, the creases crisp.

We sat at the bar like equals. I did not feel like a daughter. I doubt he felt like a dad. We were just two people who happened to find themselves in the same story. As usual, the alcohol loosened my father up, and we started to talk about my mother. He had never understood why she left. Nothing was wrong, he told me. There was no big fight. She just left.

Silence settled between us. I didn't know what to say, though I knew what I couldn't say. "She said you drank too much." "She didn't feel loved." "She didn't feel safe." At least, that's what I believed at the time. I twirled the ice around in my glass with the straw.

"It was probably for the best, though," he said. "The lifestyle I wanted really didn't have room for two kids."

He gave me a look I knew well. A boyish smile at once confessional and conspiratorial. All I could do was nod and swallow the bitter reflux of anger.

It wasn't anything I didn't already know. Kids were too messy and needy and unpredictable for my father and his second wife. With kids they couldn't stay out as late as they'd like after work, drinking at the bar with their IBM pals. They couldn't just up and go on a weekend trip. They couldn't have nice things without worrying about them getting sticky, borrowed or broken. I knew all this. Just like I knew that the only reason my father was making the effort to visit my sister was because she lived in Alaska, a place he had always wanted to visit but my stepmother did not. It wasn't to see my sister necessarily, or his two grandkids. If they had still lived in New Jersey or Indiana or South Dakota, this trip wouldn't be happening. And it wouldn't be happening without me.

A second photograph with the yellow station wagon taken along the same undisclosed part of South Carolina in late '75 or early '76 captured what I believed to be true of the dynamic between my father, my sister and me:

My mother, the snapper of the shot I assumed, zoomed in closer than my father had. And what a sad shot it was. Perhaps only because it seemed to portray what I had suspected my whole life. Of my sister and me, it was me my father was willing to fully claim as his own.

This may have been a dramatic read of the photo. But family dynamics are often dramatic, and though it was one of the old-worn narratives—"Dad liked me best"—it was, sadly, a narrative I believed was true. I wished it were not. I wished I could say my relationship with my sister had not been a snarl of clichéd rivalry. Wished I didn't have to admit how much I prized the place I felt I held in my father's regard. Wished the guilt I felt (and still feel) would assuage the pain this evidence may have caused my sister.

What I wanted to believe was that my father liked and loved both of us equally. That his reticence to show affection toward my sister was more related to his guilt of being away when she was born, of making a joke about her paternity when he came back. Or to the fact that of the two of us, my sister was the difficult one. I wanted to believe that this second picture simply captured my sister being her crabby self, that my father had tried to wrap his arms around her shoulder, and she had shrugged it away, tucking both hands under her arms to make herself unreachable.

Back to the morning in question. The morning my mother left.

In my fuzzy, fallible memory, my father was not standing stoically alone on the porch as the three of us drove off. There was a cat. And he was holding it. My sister had verified this memory. "The cat was named Casper," she had told me, "up until it had kittens in Dad's underwear drawer. Then we called her Cassie."

I found photo confirmation of the kittens. A rounded-edge snapshot dated August 1976 showed my sister and me playing with two kittens. I thought it was my sister with me in the photo, though I couldn't be sure because her head was cut off. One of the kittens was playing with my bare toes. As I looked at the photo, I could almost feel the kitten's whiskers tickling my skin.

Taking into account that the date stamp indicated development of the film and not the snapping of the photograph, it seemed safe to say that we were still at home with my father as late as August 1976.

I wanted to get the timeline right. I wanted to know the "when" so I could get to the "why." So many stories had been told in my family about this big moment: my mother leaving. So many different narratives woven. The two dominating stories were: he drank too much (hers); and she was crazy (his). It was hard to know who to trust, what to believe. Maybe if I could nail down the when—a concrete, indisputable fact, something as scientific and inarguable as how sunshine casts a shadow—then maybe I could get closer to the why. That slippery question that would hopefully lead me closer to some kind of truth.

I returned to the only clues I had: two other snapshots I found dated August 1976. In one, my father and the boy named Joey sat on a picnic table at a hotel in Myrtle Beach.

The other picture may have been taken along a stop to or from Myrtle Beach.

My sister and I stood on either side of my mother, who rested one hand on my sister's shoulder and the other on her hip. I was again out in front while my sister and mother hung back. None of us seemed to be smiling. My sister and I both squinted at the camera, our cheeks crinkled up to our eyeballs against the glaring sun. Not my mother. Her face appeared calm, unperturbed by the brightness of the day. Her lips were sealed, her jaw set, and her eyes—what was it I saw? I looked closely with my flashlight and magnifying glass—it could have been anger. Or sadness. Or exhaustion. Perhaps it was all three. She was looking off to her right. At my father or away from him? Did she know already on that summer day in '76 that she would leave him? Had she already made up her mind? Had something already made it for her?

I wondered whether my father knew. Whether he had any idea as to what might be coming in a few short months.

And what about my sister? Surely, she must have known something. "I knew about all the fighting," she told me. "But I never thought she'd leave."

There was no way to know who knew what and when. I was fairly certain I knew nothing. Of the four of us, I had the good fortune of being young and oblivious. But was I really? A memory surfaced during my gathering, of watching "Snoopy Come Home" before we left Maple Heights, of sobbing, broken-hearted, inconsolable, of my father trying to comfort me.

I didn't recall the movie at all, so I got it from the library and watched it, curious as to what about it had been so upsetting. It was a movie, I discovered, about hard choices and inevitable goodbyes. When I got to the scene where Snoopy decided to leave Charlie Brown to return to his original owner, I couldn't help but think that some part of my 3-year-old self had divined the loss that was coming. Or perhaps that was simply the moment when I became aware that loss of some kind would be unavoidable.

But who knew what when—that wasn't really the question.

One story about why my mother left was that my father slept with our babysitter. She was in many of the snapshots of those early family vacations to Myrtle Beach. In one, she was lying face down in a yellow bikini. Who else but my father would have snapped such a shot? And how did my mother feel about it? She's the one who would have placed it in one of her photo albums.

That my father was a rake was confirmed by no one less than himself. On the same night he confessed his love for the mythologized Callie Smith—that night when I was at his house on break from college—he also bestowed this gift:

"Remember that painting your mother did of the four women?" he asked me.

Of course I remembered. It was huge and gorgeous and had hung above the piano in the trailer in Florida until my mother got sick and had to go to the hospital, and all our stuff—including that painting—was stored and then burned when the storage unit caught fire. I hadn't thought about that painting since I was 10 years old.

My father puffed his pipe. "I slept with all those women."

When I recalled this conversation more than half my life later, I could smell his tobacco, could hear the tink of his pipe against the ceramic ashtray as he tapped out the ashes. What I couldn't do was find the word to describe his expression on that night as he said those words to me, his younger daughter, to whom he had no business saying them. It was definitely a smile, but what's the adjective between sheepish and shit-eating? I hated my father for this but could not tell him. How could I hate someone who was once my whole world?

It seemed a sound reason: infidelity. But I knew it couldn't be that simple.

A few years before that second confession of my father's, when I was still in high school, living with my mother—post-breakdown—in the duplex on Skyline Boulevard in Cape Coral, Florida, my mother was in the kitchen at the table drinking coffee. It could have been 8 o'clock in the morning or 8 o'clock at night. She was forever drinking coffee. A cigarette was smoldering either in the ashtray or between her fingers. She was forever smoking cigarettes. She could have been in her nightgown, a full-length short-sleeved job of cheap nylon. Her legs were probably crossed with one of them shaking, rhythmically, maddeningly. One of her boyfriends may have been at the table with us. Skip or Ron or Bobby. Maybe her soon-to-be third husband, Tom.

"I've slept with 30 men," my mother said to no one in particular. I could not imagine what we could have been talking about to warrant such a statement. She was known for such inappropriate non-sequiturs. Whether this was because of her illness or her personality, I was never able to figure out.

Could my mother simply have wanted the freedom to sow her own wild oats? To live the artistic, bohemian lifestyle she had dreamed for herself before that fateful piece of pie? Maybe.

I remembered her telling me she thought my father was a prude. And yet, he was the one cheating? None of it made any sense.

Except for my father standing alone holding that cat, I could remember nothing about the morning my mother left my father. And yet, I could imagine. I could imagine my father crying, clutching the cat to his chest, feeling sad and confused, perhaps comforted by the cat's softness and steady purr. I could imagine that first night he spent without us, him sitting in the rocking chair with the wine-colored cushion, pouring one whiskey after another, packing his pipe again and again, listening to James Taylor's "Fire and Rain" over and over on his reel-to-reel, thinking of the sunny days he thought would never end.

All of this could be true.

Or not. Maybe he spent that night drinking with friends, sloshing back and forth between tears of "I can't believe she left me" and shouts of "good riddance" before stumbling to the bed, thinking about Callie Smith and where she might have been those seven years hence.

Whatever he did that first night, I would bet my last piece of pie he got drunk.

My mother drove us from Ohio to Florida, where her parents lived. I sat on my sister's lap in the front seat much of the way, and when we had to pee, we stopped on the edge of the highway and crouched between the front and back passenger doors as cars sped by; my sister and I were afraid of the "underground toilets" at the rest stops.

"She played Kris Kristofferson the entire way down," my sister told me. "Over and over again."

I asked her if she remembered any particular song.

"Nope. She played the whole album."

I didn't know if it would have been an eight-track or a cassette. Whichever was most cutting-edge at the time; my father would have had the best. Regardless, my guess was that it was Kris Kristofferson's first album, self-titled, the one with "Me and Bobby McGee," that she played the hell out of on her long trip to a home she hoped she'd find. It was a song my father would have hated, and I could imagine her singing along in that off-key voice of hers, tearful and defiant. It was a song about dreams and heartache and unapologetic adventure. And perhaps also a song about fate and how nothing's meant to last forever. Whatever it was about, it was the kind of song a woman could leave a man to.

What was my mother feeling when she backed out of the driveway that morning? Fear, I was sure. Excitement. Doubt. How much did she feel she was running away from something, how much running toward? It couldn't have been easy. She was a young woman of 28 "without a pot to piss in," she used to say. And she had the extra baggage of two girls in tow. Her girls.

A photo I found of my sister and me on a wooden lookout, the background a rocky shoreline to some unidentified body of water somewhere between Ohio and Florida, was likely taken by my mother. It could have been right after we left my father, on the first leg of my mother's great adventure.

We had on matching jackets. Red windbreakers with white cotton lining that felt uncomfortably dry against my skin. I was squinting goofily at the camera, one of the drawstrings in my mouth. I liked to chew on the plastic tip I would one day learn was called an aglet. I looked as though I was clueless as to what was happening. As though whatever loss I may have divined from "Snoopy Come Home" had been forgotten. As though I was certain my sunny days would never end.

My sister seemed to know better. She was beside me clutching the wood railing, looking concerned and on the verge of asking a question for which there was no easy answer.

Why my mother left might have been the wrong question. Why implied that I wished my parents had stayed together. I hadn't. Had I ever wished that? I thought back. Tried to put my current self back in the mind frame of my child self, my teenage self, my young adult self.

There was a letter I wrote to my father sometime around kindergarten. I had just learned to write. It said: "Dear Daddy, I like to color. Love, Amy." I didn't remember writing it so much as I remembered being aware of its existence, though when and where I would have discovered it after writing and sending it, I didn't know. But each time I thought of it, I thought of my father and felt physical pain. Regret? Sadness? Remorse might be the best word, from the Latin "remord"—to gnaw, bite back.

Then there was a song, Randy VanWarmer's "Just When I Needed You Most." I was young when I first heard it on the soft rock station my mother listened to. How does one say it tore out my heart without sounding cliche? I must've believed my father truly loved and needed my mother, loved and needed us, his girls. Why else would I have felt such sadness? Like the letter, the song always left a mark. Every time I'd hear it, I'd instantly be pulled in; I couldn't listen without sobbing. I had the same reaction when I was 8 and 12 and 25 and 32. Up until my 45th year, that song would sink me into despair. Then I heard it on the radio and simply smiled at the memory of how inconsolable it used to make me.

And then of course there was my lone memory of the morning we left my father, of him, standing alone, clutching that damn cat. I could imagine my 4-year-old self, nose and hands pressed against the window, crying for my daddy. When I imagined it I felt so sorry, still do, regardless if it was true.

Just as likely though, I could have waved distractedly to my father as I craned my neck to watch as we backed out of the driveway. We were going on a trip, I had supposedly been told. I would've been excited. Even if I had known then that we were leaving for good, my sadness and grief would have been tempered with anticipation of what lay ahead. That's who I believed I was then—a person who knew that goodbyes were inevitable, that the only thing we could do was turn the page and embrace the next adventure.

My mother left and took us with her. That was a fact. My father was left behind. Also, a fact. Another fact: It would not have been good had they stayed together. That wasn't really a fact, just majority opinion.

Did it matter anymore why she left? I didn't know that it ever mattered. What mattered about my mother leaving was what I thought it meant then, what I thought it meant later. My mother was unhappy, or maybe just restless. She was something. My father was something else. Like so much in life, her leaving seemed to me both unavoidable and necessary. Our family, bound together more by obligation and circumstance than love, was fragile from the beginning, and I would never know what caused all the tiny fractures that led to the big break. Maybe the real question I was asking was why did it hurt so much? If we were never a whole and happy family, why had our leaving left such a mark?

An answer came to me unexpectedly one evening as I was again watching television with my husband, Aaron. The thought came so sudden and unbidden I had to believe its trueness. It's not that a promise was broken when my mother left, though many promises had been made. "I will love you forever," my father had once written to my mother. "I shall deign to prove [my love] for the rest of my living years," my mother once wrote to him. I was not so naive as to believe grand pronouncements from people so young. So no, the sadness hadn't come from promises that were broken. Rather, promise itself had been shattered. And not, as I thought, the promise of a family, but rather the promise of a father and a daughter who once were whole and happy together. That was the part of the story that gnawed at me.

Two:

1976 to 1981, Florida

Scarab Bracelet

I yowled and clutched my mother's leg, wet cheek pressed against her skirt. My grandmother pried my arms and pulled me away, angry no doubt that she was being imposed upon. I was not yet in kindergarten, so while my mother went to look for work, my grandmother was stuck with me.

"You need to do something about this child, Susan," my grandmother said, holding me tight as I squirmed and snuffled, as though my not wanting to let go of my mother was a problem.

My mother stood at the threshold of their front door, perhaps trying to convince me that she would return. But how could she console me when she was being chastised by her own mother? "You did this to yourself, Susan."

I felt like the pieces that once comprised my life were spilling out around me.

My mother left, and I continued to cry. My grandmother held a tissue to my nose and said "blow." I did.

Later, I sat on my grandmother's lap at the dining room table, and she let me fiddle with the scarabs on her bracelet. I have the bracelet still. A relic in its own right. I now know the names of each stone: black onyx, green onyx, carnelian, tiger's eye, unakite. Delicately carved in the shape of what I will one day know is the sacred beetle. Each one a symbol of a new day.

New World, New Day

Once in Florida, my mother, my sister and I stayed briefly with my grandparents in their condo in Cape Coral and then moved into a double-wide trailer in River Trails mobile home park in North Fort Myers, a city upriver from the Cape. My father and one of my uncles came down the following June to bring my mother's share of the furniture, her paintings and her piano. To my sister and me he brought white sailor hats, the first of many gifts he would give over the years, perhaps to make up for the things he wasn't able to offer.

I was so proud of that hat. It made me feel like a big girl in a big new world. At some point during my father's visit, we were driving in the van he and my uncle had driven down. I was wearing the new white sailor hat, my nickname AMY emblazoned on the brim. Wanting to show off my new hat to this new world, I stuck my head out the window. The hat promptly blew away.

It was "Snoopy Come Home" all over again. Sobbing, heartbroken, I could not be consoled. My father must have known I was not ready for another goodbye, even if it was just to a silly, souvenir hat. Perhaps that's why he pulled over onto the shoulder and, with cars whizzing by, walked back the way we had come until he found what I had so foolishly let get away from me.

According to Cuyahoga County records, my parents' divorce was final in April of 1977.

My father remarried in September of that same year.

Story had it, my father wasn't planning to get remarried when he brought his new girlfriend, Nancy, down to meet us kids. Nine years his junior, beautiful in her own right, and determined, Nancy was still living at home at the time with her parents and an older sister. She was an adventurous girl with big dreams of a big house and big cars and a big life. My handsome corporate-climbing father with his own big material dreams was her ticket out.

I found a photo that wasn't their official wedding portrait. It was likely taken the day after or the day before. They were wearing the same clothes as in the official portrait, but their hairstyles were different, my father's hair in dire need of combing. Like the other pictures I gathered, it seemed to show so distinctly what I had suspected for 40 years: Nancy wanted my father all to herself. Other than a few and fleeting gooey moments of questionable sincerity—"You girls have never appreciated how much I love you"—I never felt loved by Nancy.

The composition intrigued me. My father stood rigid with his left shoulder situated in such a way it appeared his left arm might have been hanging just as passively at his side as his right one. But, no. Upon closer inspection, I could see—just barely— the tips of his fingers around Nancy's waist. While Nancy (bold girl!) embraced him firmly. Was she embracing him? Gripping him? Latching on to him? Whatever the verb to describe the action, it was an act of will. She stared straight into the camera, as if saying in simple terms with those piercing brown eyes: "He's mine."

My father looked to the side with an expression that might have been grim or shyly happy. How had he felt about finding himself in yet another seemingly hasty marriage? Was he looking away because he felt embarrassed? Ashamed? Or was he looking at my sister and me? Very likely we would've been there as well. Was he wanting to speak up and invite us into the frame? There was room for two young girls in the shot; that is, if we all were willing to squeeze in close.

My sister and I both thought Nancy was pretty when we met her that fall, with her deep brown eyes and round face that lit up when she smiled. It was a smile that would not often shine on us, but I'm sure on that day, our first meeting, she smiled broadly and gave us each a big hug when we were introduced. Nancy was never shy. And she would've kissed us both on the cheek and rubbed at the pink lipstick stain with her fingertips afterwards. This kissing and leaving her mark, her signature gesture. The pretense of rubbing it off or in (who could be sure?) would confuse us for decades.

They were staying at the Lani Kai, a resort on Fort Myers Beach that would become their Myrtle Beach. There was one photograph I found of my sister, Nancy, and me posing on the balcony during that visit, the Gulf of Mexico behind us. We were all smiling like we should. As I looked at the photograph, I could still smell Nancy's perfume, sharp and sweet, different from my mother's musky scent. Nancy was taller than my mother. Taller than my father too, by inches, a fact she never tried to hide. Though whoever took the unofficial wedding portrait hid it well enough.

I never knew the details as to how they decided to elope at The Little Chapel by the Sea. Had my father wanted to get married again so soon? It wouldn't have mattered. Vietch once told me of the day he first met Nancy, "I told your dad he didn't stand a chance with that one." Perhaps my father was afraid another woman would leave him if he didn't give in and say yes.

My sister and I were at the wedding ceremony. I didn't recall having any concept of what was happening. I doubted I had been upset; they had given us candy at the end. "I was upset," my sister told me. "I remember telling Nancy that Dad had seen Mom naked, hoping to get under her skin." As my sister recalled, Nancy coolly replied, "Well, I certainly hope so!"

The following summer, my sister and I returned to Ohio. I recalled flying there, our first flight ever. I could imagine my young self in the window seat with the little plastic airline wings pinned to my top, tugging at my sister's sleeve excitedly.

"Look!" I could imagine saying, pointing to the shimmering lights below. "We're above the stars!"

But there was photo confirmation to the contrary: a snapshot of my father, my sister and me posing in front of a brick wall. On my sister's shirt was what looked like a United Airlines sticker, slanted red and white stripes with the stylized U logo. On the back my father had written: "Sami and Amy at the airport after their first flight from Florida." The date stamp read July 1979, a full year later.

So in 1978, we had likely been driven to Ohio. My father would probably have driven down with his friend Danny or one of my uncles to pick us up. I had a vague memory of a brown and white van and Danny's sons riding along, if not on that drive, then another. The boy closest to my age sat with his legs open nearly the entire trip so I could see his genitals poking out of his shorts. You don't forget a thing like that.

My father drove 1,200 miles just to pick us up. Then another 1,200 miles to take us back to Ohio. If you factor in he had to drive us back to Florida and then himself back to Ohio, that's 4,800 miles. Eighty hours of his life. For us. His girls.

His dedication was … what was an adequate word? Astounding. From the Middle English "astone"—to stun, to strike senseless with a blow.

His dedication was astounding.

I was sad it hadn't been more memorable, that it took me four decades to consider it. My father, at least in the summer of '78, was as adept at fatherhood as any child could hope.

I couldn't remember that first visit itself but found two pictures that were taken upon our arrival at our grandparents' house in Norwalk. I expected to see "home" in the welcome sign my grandparents must have made. But it was not there. After the divorce, my sister and I would never come home again. Instead, we would dress up in clothes we usually wouldn't wear and simply visit.

Despite all that had happened, in the photos, none of us looked the worse for wear. It was 1978, according to the date on the back. Almost two years after my mother left with us headed to Florida. On the back of the shot of the three of us, probably contemporaneous with it, I had written: "Me and Sam at my Grandma Hoyts house." The writing had the sloppy quality of a hand just learning. Even under the scrutiny of my magnifying glass, we looked happy, our smiles candid. My sister's hand rested easily and familiarly on my father's shoulder, while his hands held on to each of us. These were three people who belonged together. Who wanted to be together.

But that welcome sign. The omission of the word home. To him, with him, we would forever be guests.

Guests or not, I recalled fond memories of those early visits. It was during those visits that my father began teaching us the art of stained glass. Being in his workshop, being there with him, is still one of the happiest memories I have of the three of us. One reason was Nancy never ventured there. While the rest of the house was her domain, my father had carved out a place just for himself. In his workshop, my sister and I could have him to ourselves. He was relaxed there, as relaxed as he ever could be without being tipsy. Joking with us about untying our belly buttons so our butts would fall off. Singing the wrong lines to songs on purpose to make us giggle. Sometimes, he'd put his arm around one of our shoulders and give a squeeze. While my sister likely shrunk away from such affection, I would nestle in, feeling almost as though I had never left.

The disconnect my sister and I felt with our parents in Maple Heights continued with our mother in North Fort Myers. She worked full time, so wasn't around much during the week. But even when she was, she wasn't. Her parents had been strict and overbearing; she believed children needed to experience the world on their own, make their own mistakes. She had few rules: don't use the word butthole ("that's gross"); don't watch "Welcome Back, Kotter" ("that's idiotic"); don't say the N-word, even if the neighbors do ("that's not who we are"). She made chore lists, and my sister made sure I helped abide them, vacuuming and dusting and emptying the overflowing ashtrays on a weekly basis. We lugged the laundry to the laundromat behind our trailer, near the pool, and searched the machines for loose change. We gave each other rides in the big metal clothes carts, wobbly wheels gliding over the linoleum, carefree shrieks punctuating the tumbly rumbling of the dryers, before we crashed into the wall with a definitive thud. "My turn! My turn!"

Though my sister was with me more than my mother, I was most often alone. I had one friend before the first grade, a girl named Cheryl who lived across the street in a single-wide trailer with her parents and their dog. Her dad crushed beer bottle caps with one hand and called her "Fat Baby." When I wasn't with her playing Barbies or making perfectly round mud pies near her hose spigot, I was by myself.

The trailer park was a sprawling community of mostly run-down mobile homes with front yards of scrubby grass and sand spurs. The pond we passed on our shortcut to the bus stop was home to a gator that ate its weight in dogs and cats and other small things unfortunate enough to get too close. There was a pavilion covered in the crude graffiti of bored teenagers and a playground complete with swing set and merry-go-round. There was also a rare shade-giving tree near the playground in which my sister and her friends once built a tree house.

From the satellite view online, the main Suwanee Drive ran like a river for nearly a mile, with dead-end side roads shooting off like perpendicular tributaries. How many days had I spent wandering those roads?

One day I wandered alone with an empty coffee can. I was out to collect parts for some grand machine. I didn't know what. Maybe I'd make a TV that I could star on to replace the cardboard box TV I'd already made with a cut-out screen and crayoned-on knobs. Maybe a rocket ship, since the refrigerator box I had found outside and converted never would lift off. I'd have to wait and see what I could find. I spent the whole day plucking bolts and screws and miscellaneous pieces of sturdy plastic out of the dirt. I collected loose springs and washers and lengths of string. Anything that looked like it had once been part of something else, I put in my can.

Back at the trailer, on the screened-in side porch, I dumped out what I had gathered onto my cardboard box desk. The smell was gritty and metallic. Giddy with expectation, but also focused, intent, I felt on the verge of some new and beautiful thing. With no plan, no blueprint, no idea of what I might build, I started connecting the pieces and the parts. This bolt in that nut. String through a washer. I studied the shapes of the various plastic bits to see where they might fit, held a loose spring in my hand. "Where do you go?"

Nothing came of any of it, but I wasn't disappointed. There had been satisfaction in the bringing together of all those discarded things. I put everything back in the coffee can. Then, with grimy hands, I shuffled pieces of scrap paper my mother had brought home from her job at the printing press, and behind the cut-out screen of my cardboard TV, I shared my news with the world.

During those days, I was a child all wobbly and carefree, exploring and experiencing my world. But then the nights would come like definitive thuds. I couldn't sleep.

My sister and I shared a room, a twin bed each. I fared better when I could sleep with her in her bed, but she didn't always like me to. I was a gross kid. I picked my nose and wiped the boogers on the wall, delighting in her disgust. I was also an affectionate kid. I wanted to snuggle and spoon, but my sister didn't like to be touched, especially not by my boogered hands.

So most nights I stayed in my bed, awake, wondering when it was going to be 10 o'clock and hoping I'd be asleep before then. I couldn't go ask my mother what time it was, or crawl into her bed and spoon up against her warmth. She almost always had a boyfriend, living in or staying over, who took up her attention.

I have no idea why 10 o'clock was such a looming hour, but I feared it more than any monster under my bed. It was when the world shut down. Everyone would be asleep, soundly dreaming their dreams, and I would be alone. It was one thing to be by yourself with the world going on around you. But if you were to be caught by yourself without the world … that would be something akin to annihilation. I didn't know such a big word then, but I felt its power, sensed the gaping maw of nothingness that was waiting to disappear me.

Blanket pulled high over my head, fear hot on my skin, I'd close my eyes tight, get as still as I could, and hope the nothingness would not find me.

And then, before I knew it, I'd awake to a new day.

Mom, Before

I was entranced by the satellite view I found online of our old home in River Trails. Everything was so familiar. There was our trailer, near the front, the community pool in our backyard. Across the street from our trailer lived a woman named Madeline and her dog, who barked and barked and barked until the gator got him. Down Suwanee Drive at the road you'd turn onto if you were driving to the pool, a woman named Mabel lived on the corner. She weighed 800 pounds and would call out as someone passed. Sometimes, with my sister, I'd go in and get candy.

You could cut through Madeline's yard—past Kelly T.'s trailer, past the road where Tina S. and her brother Shannon lived—and get to the bus stop. My sister had a crush on Shannon's friend Clyde. She thought he was a babe. He was friends with Johnny C. They all knew a girl named Yvonne who went out with an older guy named Beanie. I used to do an impression of Beanie, just a simple crotch-grab with a drawled out "yuk-yuk" that used to make my sister and Yvonne laugh. In the back of the park, my best friend, Heather, who I met in the first grade, lived in a double-wide with her parents and older brother. My sister's best friend lived in the back of the park, too. Our best friends were both named Heather, so there was little Heather and big

Heather. When Amy B., a girl my sister's age, moved in across from Kelly T., we became known as little Amy and big Amy.

So many memories from those six years: games of kick the can; dumpster diving with little Heather, carting our treasures away on her granny's trike; falling into Cheryl's front yard cactus—the thing as big as a car—and howling as her mom plucked the spines from my skin; getting yelled at by Joyce, the park's manager, for not wearing our bathing caps in the pool; gorging on the small sour oranges that grew in somebody's backyard; catching minnows in the puddles in front of big Heather's trailer; going door-to-door to collect money to help the family whose trailer burnt down; trick-or-treating until our pillow cases sagged and we could barely dump them out onto the living room floor when we got home.

The memories came in a rush. I wondered why I couldn't remember as much about my mother. "Maybe that's how we dealt with her getting sick," my sister said. "Maybe to accept she was gone we had to act like we never had her."

I found that I remembered my mother in those days in the same way I remembered the blue velour sofa she's sitting on in the photograph: They were things I had always had in my world and thought I always would.

The blue velour sofa was much bluer in my memory than in the photo. An afghan laid along the back. I wondered who'd made it. Certainly not my mother. Or hers. Possibly my mother's grandmother, Great Grandma Wyss. My mother was sentimental. She liked homemade things. In the photo she looked a little drunk, but that was unlikely; my mother was not a drinker. Unless the picture was taken around Christmas. Then, it was quite possible the empty glass she was holding in her right hand had a Kahlúa and cream in it. It would only have taken one to give her that tipsy look. But a thick drink like that would likely have left a film, and the glass looked clear. My guess was Kool-Aid or sun tea.

The photo appeared to have been taken at night. She was sitting in front of the living room window with the curtains drawn. If it were daytime, my mother, then, would've let the sun in. A lamp off-camera cast its light to her right. Who took the picture? Her live-in boyfriend of several years? The young guy who taught my sister how to do one-handed push ups? Earl Brack? I didn't think the picture was of the Earl Brack era, that is, the breakdown era. I had other pictures of my mother during that time, and her curly hair was much longer then, long enough to put in a bun. Her hair in this shot was just above her shoulders.

My guess was the picture was taken soon after the divorce. She was perhaps not even a year free from her first marriage. She looked young and chirpy, her adventure so far, a success. She had her girls and a job and people to smile at. Her whole life was ahead of her.

I tried to call to mind this pre-breakdown mother, but all I got were the old, played-out memories. The sound of rings clattering against piano keys. How she'd nod at me when it was time to turn the page. The feel of her soft, wooly hair. The smell of cigarette smoke and suntan oil. The rich color of her favorite blue terry cloth jumper.

With a little more concentration, I conjured other things. The contents of her top dresser drawer: silk slips with fraying hems; underwear with dark crotch stains; pantyhose in a myriad of shades. The mess of make-up strewn across her bathroom counter: sticky bottles of foundation; stray false eyelashes; unsharpened eyebrow pencils. The treasure trove that was her jewelry box: bangle bracelets in silver and bronze; necklaces made of rope and beads; turquoise rings; scrimshaw pendants my sister made for her.

Those things didn't really get to the heart of who she was, though. Or rather, of who we were to each other.

Some 20 years after her death, my mother pre-breakdown, that is, "before," seemed illusory. Like the wedding portrait of her and my father, the image I carried of her in my mind from this era of my life was of something wished for, but never achieved. She was always just beyond reach.

I considered a family portrait, this portrait from before, taken at an Olan Mills, circa 1979 or '80.

The three of us were set against a black backdrop. My mother's left hand rested near, but not on, my left arm. My sister stood—always at the ready—behind us. There were no hands upon shoulders or arms wrapped around waists. I, a child of abundant affection, was not snuggled up close to my mother; I was not even leaning back onto my sister. Whose choice was it to position us in this way? Three beings, together but alone, amid emptiness.

My mother was stunning in the photograph. Her naturally curly dark brown hair—frosted and feathered, full of body and perfectly styled—fell just above her shoulders. It was as soft as it looked and was not the only thing frosted. Her eyelids, her lips and her jewelry all seemed to shimmer. Her skin, in contrast, was bronzed. There was coolness to her beauty, there was warmth. Her eyes, to me, looked sad. I wished she was smiling. Her cheekbones, as I've said, were made for smiling.

My sister was probably 11 in the photo. Her eyes—froggy without makeup, the adult her would say—were strong and direct. Her smile was close-lipped, a little snarky—she hated pictures. She was pale and unadorned, wearing a white country western-style blouse that did nothing to compliment her complexion or her personality. She was a feisty, angry girl prone to fits of kindness, like baking me cookies or buying small plastic animals for my menagerie. The pink elephant was my favorite.

I was a tan maybe 8-year-old. I must have been instructed to try to look serious. Or at least subdued. The image revealed the effort it took—all the muscles around my mouth and up into my cheeks were engaged, ready to break into a smile. I wore a hand-me-down dress of my sister's, dusky blue and drapey, still a good two sizes too big. A dainty gold necklace with three oblong pearly stones dangled around my neck. It was a gift for my birthday, a day I shared with my mother, which means she might have been 32.

In the photograph, then, we were possibly only a year away from what we will forever call her breakdown.

I looked at my mother, so poised and put together. Coiffed is a word she would've used. She didn't look real. She looked made up. Did we make her up? Did this before mother ever exist?

The other photographs I had of her, of us, during this time were few and only showed a glimpse, and that of someone I didn't fully recognize. I concentrated hard, bidding the memories to come, hoping a solid image of her would materialize.

Some things I recalled easily. How my sister and I would rub her feet after a day spent in work heels, then tickle her until she almost peed her pants. How I'd cup her cheeks with my hands and give her butterfly kisses. How she warned us when we sassed that she got us from a pack of gypsies, and if we didn't shape up, she'd ship us right back. How she'd make us tea and toast and put frozen washcloths on our foreheads when we were feeling sick. How she blamed us for her small breasts. "I had a nice chest before you two ruined me." I could say with certainty that she was funny and kind and easy to be around.

I could also say with certainty that she was embarrassing and uninvolved. How she told everyone about me walking in on her and her live-in boyfriend having sex. "Amy saw her first bare butt." How she would let us practically do anything unattended, unsupervised. "Why don't you go blow the stink off yourselves," she'd say, urging us out of the house. How I didn't feel I could go to her all those nights when I couldn't sleep.

But those were mere fragments, bits of dialogue. Not enough to craft a scene.

The few memories I had of us interacting were hardly remarkable as far as I could tell. But maybe there was a reason they surfaced.

The first: I was about 6 years old and at the tennis court with her. I was at the fence when she came over to retrieve a wayward ball. As she bent down to pick it up, I started to climb, my fingers curling around the thin, metal links. She cried out suddenly and I laughed and kept climbing. I thought she was trying to be funny, like she often was, making silly faces and sounds to make us laugh. She grimaced, waved her hand and pointed downward as I started to bounce, still thinking it was a game. Then I looked down and realized her foot was caught under the fence. I was hurting her.

I felt bad, but also something else. Something difficult to name. Distant perhaps. Or maybe the word I wanted was detached. I didn't recall rushing toward her to console or soothe. There was only my mother, her eyes closed, sucking air through gritted teeth. And me, feeling ashamed as I mumbled "Sorry," and shrunk into myself.

Could the feeling have been fear? Could I have been afraid that if I hurt her, she would leave me, too?

Another: We were at Murray's Country Store on Slater Road. My mother was buying milk. On the magazine rack near the door, I spied a Huey, Duey and Luey coloring book. I wanted that book. My mother said no, gently. She may have tried to explain how she only had money for the milk. I didn't care. In front of my mother and the world, I stomped my small feet, balled up my hands, and let out a wail loud enough to reach Ohio. It always felt good to throw a big fit, and that day at Murray's the fit paid off; I got my coloring book. Though looking back I felt bad for being such a brat, I liked this memory, for it showed a typical scene between mother and child.

Many of the memories of my mother, before, came to me in remnants and wisps that were similar enough to piece together into composite scenes.

Like this: Being at the park's pool behind our double-wide. The slapping sound of wet feet on concrete, cacophony of radios, the shrieks of other children. My mother lounged on a chair, beads of sweat on her tanned skin, and pulled the top of her suit away to check the line. She smelled of coconut oil and cigarettes. "Come rub some of this on my back, Amy," she said, handing me the dark bottle. It was slippery in my hand. Her skin was smooth and firm beneath my small fingers as I swirled the oil around in random patterns.

And this: Going out on my grandfather's boat on the Caloosahatchee River. The roar of the engine, the chop of the waves. Gulls swooping overhead, determined to be seen if they couldn't be heard. As the boat pitched, so did my stomach. My mother, her arms glistening with droplets of spray, held me tight on her lap, calming my queasy belly.

There was photographic evidence of at least one such boat outing.

The picture seemed to be from the era shortly after the divorce, still early into this new life full of possibility. I dated the photo by my outfit, which I remembered distinctly. I had several such outfits in kindergarten that made me feel professional. Playing secretary by myself with papers dug out of my grandfather's office trash can was one of my favorite pastimes. So, I must have been 5 or 6 years old. The back of my grandfather's head appeared in the image, while my mother and I were in the foreground looking to our right. I was on her lap but leaning forward, away from her. The water in the background was calm; I had no need for her arms. My mother was still young, still chirpy, smiling easily, warmly. I had my eyes closed, my back to her. It seemed I was a child who trusted that her mother would be there for her when the waters got choppy. I had no reason to believe, then, that one day she would not be.

None of those memories—neither the singular nor the composite, neither the happy nor the sad—made me feel warm and fuzzy or any closer to "us." Thinking about my mother, before, left me feeling squirrelly, a word she used to use, post-breakdown. A word I understood to mean uneasy for unknown reasons. There was still something between us I couldn't identify.

Really though, couldn't I? Wasn't the thing looming between us obvious?

I had been trying to capture an image of my mother before by looking back from after. Of course she wasn't going to look the same. The picture of her would forever be obscured, as any image would be, seen through the cracked glass of mental illness.

Maybe my sister was right. Maybe it was best not to remember how wonderful a mother she was. Maybe it was best not to remember how she used to laugh at my stupid impressions (of Fred Sanford, of Carol Burnett), or how she hid our Easter baskets every year, or how she kept us well-stocked in colorful paper from her job at Press Printing, or how she called us affectionately by nicknames (Jakey Begonia for my sister, Ruby Begonia for me). Maybe it was best I couldn't remember her tucking us in or telling us she loved us. For if we ever had that before, we did not have it after.

Three:

1981 to 1982, Florida

Mad Lib

My best friend, Heather, was in the bathtub while I sat on the toilet. We were playing Mad Libs. We were both 9 years old. Heather was scrappy but small, and in the tub with her head plastered with dark wet hair and her chest flat and white, she looked especially tiny.

We were laughing at some silly arrangement of words when my mother appeared in the doorway, like an apparition, cigarette smoldering between her fingers. I waited for her to say something. To ask what we were doing, were we going to come watch TV, would we like some popcorn. But she didn't speak. She simply stared at Heather, whose mouth was gaping open mid-laugh. The silence was thick. Consuming. It felt like that maw of nothingness I feared would disappear me late at night. I stayed still. Waiting. A drop of water eventually dripped from the tub faucet. Then another. None of us moved.

Finally, my mother spoke to me, but with her eyes on Heather. "Be careful when you pull the drain. She'll go right down." Then, in a cloud of smoke, she disappeared.

"What the fuck?" said my tiny, scrappy friend.

When I examined my mother's words as an adult, they seemed innocuous, almost funny. But it was the tone that got me, and Heather too. I would search for an adjective to fill in the blank of that new space. Perhaps "irresonant"—a strange and fitting word for such a dead, flat sound.

Silence Descends

T he period between the before and the after—what my family always called "the breakdown"—was a quiet affair. If there was anything unquiet about it, time had dampened the sound. My memory of that short era was split in two. I remembered a great deal that occurred outside of the trailer, where part of my life was going along as normal, but next to nothing that occurred inside the trailer, where the other part of my life was not.

I didn't know when my mother's breakdown happened. Did it start before Christmas or after? Was it gradual or sudden? I vaguely recalled my mother telling me she was in the kitchen when she felt something shift irrevocably inside of her. But I couldn't be certain that was true. She also told me about a day I came home breathless and excited about something I had done at school. "You handed me this piece of paper and I just crumpled it up. Right in front of your face." I didn't remember that at all. Not one whiff of it. My sister didn't recall much, either. "I knew something wasn't right with her," she told me. "I remember I took advantage and got her to buy me some new shoes."

I didn't even remember that Christmas. Was that the year I got the Crayola Caddy? Was that the year my mother forgot to put our stocking stuffers in our stockings, and my sister and I had to tell her where she had hid them? Did we string popcorn? Sing songs? Had things already started to fall apart?

Here's what I knew:

I was in the fourth grade and my teacher was Mr. W. He had been my sister's fourth grade teacher, and he and my mother were friendly; they may have even slept together. He was a thin, mustachioed man who wouldn't let the black girl in our class use the "bafroom" until she said it in "English" and who often addressed his own son as "you little faggot." But he was devoted to me, my sister and my mother, who he referred to as "his girls."

I was in a gifted program called Major Work Area, in which I got to do projects of my own choosing. According to that year's Individual Education Plan I was "very prolific," completing projects on Abe Lincoln, Buffalo Bill Cody, cannibals, witchcraft and medieval armor. Where on earth in 1981 does a 9-year-old find information on cannibals?

MTV was born that year and HBO started offering 24-hour scheduling. The world was crazy for the Rubik's Cube, which I could never figure out how to solve. I liked "Choose Your Own Adventure" books and wore my hair either in high pigtails or pinned back with purple barrettes shaped like Crayola crayons. By my 10th birthday in April, we lived with my grandparents, and my sister gave me a thin purple headband as a gift. She left it on my dinner plate. My sister was always good at surprising me.

I was in a tinikling show at the Edison Pageant of Light in Fort Myers. I didn't know then that tinikling was a traditional Philippine dance; I thought of it as jump rope with sticks. Memory told me I was the dancer, the one who jumped over and between the clattering bamboo poles. But I could have been one of the clappers, rhythmically moving the poles in time with another kid: tap, tap, slide; tap, tap, slide. The only thing I remembered for certain was I had poison oak all over my face the day of the pageant. I thought I looked like the Elephant Man, from the movie I had just seen on HBO at Heather's house. I had gotten the poison oak from playing pirates and shipwreck in the woods near the bus stop with Heather. A certificate from the pageant was dated Feb. 13.

So, the actual breaking down—or at least the level of breakage necessitating intervention by my grandparents—must have been sometime between February and April 1982.

I discovered boys that year. Mark was in my class. We were boyfriend and girlfriend for about three days. He gave me a ceramic brooch with an image of a man and woman in a garden. I still had it as of this writing, though the pin had long fallen off. How did such a thing survive the journey of nearly 40 years? Judging by the woman's full skirt, the man's floppy hat and leggings, the figures appeared to be 18th century. In the parlance of those long-ago days, they were "making love." Mark and I talked on the phone once. I made the call from my mother's bedroom, having the distinct feeling—not for the first time—that boys were going to want something from me soon, but not really knowing what that something was going to be.

Another boy, also in my class, Greg, was an immigrant kid whose family were traveling circus performers. I was crazy about him ... for about six hours. I spent an entire day fantasizing about running away with him and his trapeze-flying family, having babies who would have Greg's thick Eric Estrada hair and game show host smile. By the end of the school day, I felt sick at the thought of ever having a baby and couldn't stand the sight of poor Greg.

My first big crush, though, was Matt Martell. He rode my bus and lived down a dirt road outside of River Trails. He wore dark bootlegged jeans—Tuffys, probably—and button-down shirts with pearl buttons. Sometimes, a ball cap with a Confederate flag. He had short dark hair and long eyelashes. A quiet manner I read as kind. He was in the fifth grade. I never spoke to him. He never once looked at me that I could remember. But I loved him more than any other boy. I would always love him, the boy I never knew, the boy who never knew me. My mythologized boy. My wished-for boy.

I remembered only a few things about my mother during the year of the breakdown. She was working on the mural in the children's room at the Science of Mind Center. I caught literal whiffs of the building as I recalled it. The clean, empty smell of conditioned air. The tangy scent of paint. And a tactile memory: the feel of a brush in my hand as I painted squiggly feet on ladybugs.

She played piano at the center during services sometimes. There was a photo of the two us one Sunday morning, just before.

She had on her most beautiful dress, a light purple satin job with lace trim. The song would have been "Let There Be Peace on Earth," maybe "Amazing Grace." And there was an ashtray. I had a light purple dress on, too. My hair, up like hers, though my jewelry consisted of only a plastic digital watch. I wanted to be just like her, at least on that day. I wondered who snapped the picture. Who was I looking at, so serious? I remembered distinctly feeling proud and grown up. But when I examined it later, across the course of half a lifetime, my 9-year-old self looked more pensive than proud. I couldn't help feeling my younger self was conveying a message to me, telling me something she had intuited already at her young age: "This is one of the last moments we'll have like this."

I remembered so little about what happened inside the trailer during that year, that spring. It was as though the pieces of glass comprising the picture of our life together in that place at that time were so crushed that the color and quality were no longer discernible.

There were only two remaining memories of the breaking down:

In the first, I was in the driveway of the trailer about to get into my grandparents' car. I was clutching a spiral notebook in which I was writing a novel. It was about a young girl like me who fell into a heavy crush with a much older boy named Clayton. She had an older sister who was mean and a mother who would soon be crazy. I wrote in rounded, vertical cursive. The letters plump and happy looking. It was a story I would eventually abandon, not knowing how to end it.

In the second, I was in my grandparents' white Toyota. Was it the same day? I didn't know. My grandfather was driving. My grandmother sat stiffly in the passenger's seat. I was in the back with my mother, as far away from her as I could get, shoulder pressed against the door. The glass of the window cool against my cheek. My mother was smiling and laughing to herself. Sometimes she'd ask my grandparents a question that made no sense. Then she'd nod in a knowing way and laugh some more.

Examining these memories, I had my own questions. Where were we going? Where was my sister? Though, then, the most pressing question was: What was this new thing settling in between us all, so thick and stifling it was hard to even breathe?

In July of 1993, the summer before my senior year of college, I wrote what I imagined may have happened in the spring of '82:

"I could feel our air begin to collapse as she took heavy, frantic drags on her cigarette and nervously thumbed the mole on her cheek. The seconds ticked. Slowly. Slowly. Until they almost stood still.

Everything comes to a halt. Time and my mother stop breathing. For a critical moment I think this is death. I become more and more frightened by the intensity of her silence. Telling me more than she'd like to say, revealing more than I want to know. The panic seizes me as if to choke the breath out of me, too, and I run to embrace her, hoping that the reality of her nearness will quell the fear surging through my body.

But I can do nothing but shake her, hoping to bring her out of this frightening stupor, thinking naively that by sheer will alone I can make it all go away. In the end I just cry. For everything I don't understand. For everything I will never know."

I found the tone of my 20-something self to be melodramatic, and her careless shifts in tense embarrassing; but she described that annihilating silence to a tee.

One thing about our home life endured in my memory—rather, one person: Earl Brack. Though in truth, it was not really Earl himself who had retained his clarity. No, he himself faded with time; only vague recollections of him remained. How he brought me two-liter bottles of pop and bags of candy when he came over, sometimes packs of Hubba Bubba. And I recalled him having short hair, and shirts with his name stitched on the pocket. I could just see the white thread script.

What remained fixed and indelible was the idea of him. The mythology of him. For Earl Brack was the man credited by my mother, my sister and me for making my mother go crazy. I said credit, not blame because in the Oxford English Dictionary, "credit" in the general sense meant "to take as true or truthful," which was most fitting. The three of us took it to be true that Earl Brack was the root cause of my mother's sickness.

In the autumn of 1981 when Earl was still coming around, things were pretty right in my world. I felt solidly and unthinkingly at home in our double-wide, where, in the kitchen, bugs the size of my hand flew around and hissed. Where, in the second bathroom, rats had gnawed through the linoleum. And where, in the living room, ants nested in the color television. When my friends and I played hide and seek, I would peel back a sheet of paneling in the hall closet and hide in the wall.

The trailer had air-conditioning, new carpet, windows that let in the light, and pale blue kitchen cabinets I always thought so unique and pretty. The blue velour couch and lone puzzle table from Maple Heights shared space with a wicker table and chair, while the walls gave room for my mother's paintings. Against one wall, my mother's piano. Next to the turntable, propped on a shelf, albums that filled the air with music. Kenny Rogers and Roger Whitaker. Eddie Rabbitt, Seals and Crofts. KC and the Sunshine Band. On a bookcase, next to "The Clan of the Cave Bear," "Linda Goodman's Sun Signs" and Ernest Holmes' "The Science of Mind," my mother kept three astrological charts, each one of our destinies—hers, mine, my sister's—bound in hard blue plastic. What I wouldn't have given to unearth those relics.

My favorite place in the trailer was the bedroom I shared with my sister. She didn't spend much time in our bedroom on weekend nights during this time. She was usually out with her friends, doing her own things that did not involve me. My mother spent weekend nights in her own bedroom with Earl Brack doing things I imagined were similar to what Cheryl and I made our Barbie and Ken dolls do. Grown-up things that involved taking off their clothes and grinding their crotches together.

In my room, I had a small black and white television, and on it I watched "The Dukes of Hazzard," "The Incredible Hulk," "Dallas." In my memory of this time, it was perpetually Friday night. I drank pop from a plastic cup and stuffed myself with candy. I ate as much as I wanted. I never got sick. I felt safe and happy and whole, albeit a little uneasy when the music from my mother's room stopped and I heard Earl's car pull away into the night.

Earl Brack existed and was a married man, that much was fact. Everything else about Earl Brack was suspect. One story was he promised my mother he would leave his wife, and when he didn't, my mother was so distraught, she lost her mind. Another story was he gave my mother pot to smoke, and she had a bad reaction that made her lose her mind. Yet another was my mother was so reckless and wild and promiscuous, that made her lose her mind. In every version of the story that tried to answer why my mother went crazy, Earl Brack had something to do with it.

Even years later, when my mother was somewhat stable and remarried to her third and final husband, Earl Brack would surface again in a new story explaining why my mother got sick. She went to a past life regression treatment and recounted the experience to me in a letter.

April 16, Mon.

Dear Amy:

Well, yesterday I did it. I went for a past-life regression. And I learned a few interesting things. In one life my name was Harry and I was a Lieutenant in the U.S. Calvary in Colorado. Harry killed an Indian woman and then was haunted by dreams about her all his life. Under hypnosis I looked into the Indian's eyes and saw ███████████'s soul. After Harry killed the Indian because she did not love him, he asked his Captain to recruit out of the Calvary and went to live in a cabin with his dog. One day Harry went out to find his dog, during the winter, and got his foot caught in a trap and froze to death. In another scene I was Sharon Rose and I ran a boarding house for men on San Francisco's waterfront. I was in love with a seagoer named Michael. He said he loved Rose, but he was always going to sea and he died at sea leaving Rose to age quickly and die alone with only her Negro slave and a little girl at her bedside. The hypnotist said ████ and I had a Karmic bond and that I broke it in this lifetime, because I did not get angry at him this time and kill him. Instead I chose to make myself sick in this lifetime, thus breaking the Karma that surrounded Harry's demise. Very interesting. Another interesting thing. When I looked at the man named Michael under hypnosis I was seeing Tom's past life and that we were bonded spiritually and that in essence he didn't leave me when he died at sea, instead he re-manifested in this life as Tom so we could be together this time. The whole session took an hour and a half and I was fully conscious the whole time, although in a light hypnotic state. Believe it or not Amy I cried and got angry at myself for making myself sick in this lifetime. The counselor said I was perhaps still feeling Harry's rage from a previous incarnation. Also, after the session I felt light headed and much relieved. Someday I am going back to see if another session won't reveal even more past lives. The session really made me see why in this life I adore men and dislike women and that also explains why I felt such a bond with ████. I killed him the last time. Tom sat through the session with me and he said he found it really enlightening.

Earl Brack was as good an explanation as any. The others were no better: That my grandmother was cold and unnurturing—a "schizophrenogenic mother" (a mother-blaming theory that was still espoused as late as the late 1980s in encyclopedias I consulted in high school); or that my mother had a defect of character, was weak-willed and unable to handle the responsibilities of raising two children (a theory likely espoused by my grandparents); or that my mother had a chemical imbalance in her brain, too much dopamine in this part, too little in that one (this was the most recent dominating theory). None of those explanations satisfied the need I felt at 9 and 12 and 15, 28 or even closing in on 50, as to why my mother got sick and what she got sick with.

In 1997, I wrote this in a journal:

"941 is the area code of Arcadia, Florida. Tried calling that hospital my mom was in but couldn't remember the name of it. Made me feel good and creepy asking for it. Just calling information was chilling. Like channeling the spirits. Trying to communicate with another world."

It occurred to me later I could have asked my mother the name of the hospital—she was alive then. But how could I have explained to her why knowing the name was important to me when I didn't even know myself? Memory told me I got the name in '97 and called the hospital and requested medical records. But I was sure my memory was wrong. My journal was more reliable, and it didn't mention anything of the sort.

In the early 2000s, when I finally had access to the Internet and was able to Google "state mental hospital in Arcadia, Florida," I discovered the name: G. Pierce Wood Memorial Hospital. Again, memory wanted to tell me I called and requested medical records, maybe sent an email. But again, I thought my memory was wrong. A decade or so later, I would find information on the hospital's opening and closing (1947 and 2002, respectively). And in 2020, with little hope of ever discovering more about the hospital in which my mother was briefly held, I stumbled upon a website called Abandoned Florida, with a whole section on G. Pierce Wood, complete with color photographs.

I wish I was blown away by this discovery. That I felt overwhelming excitement or sadness or relief or something. Abandoned Florida? How could I not find that uncanny? And yet, I didn't feel much but tempered curiosity. In my 20s and 30s, when I was still prone to melodrama, before I was a psychiatric nurse, I would likely have looked at the photographs through the lens of "Cuckoo's Nest," imagining all manner of horrors and terrors: straitjackets; mind control; lobotomies; insulin comas; starvation; isolation. Having since been exposed to many psychiatric units, albeit from behind the nurses' station, I imagined that G. Pierce Wood, at least by the 1980s, was much more mundane, a non-bedlam of chemically-restrained people shuffling their way down dark and lonely hallways. Maybe that was why I didn't feel as squirrelly as I thought I would.

I didn't know if my sister and I were ever taken to G. Pierce Wood, though my emotional memory said we were, at least once. I had the vaguest memory of a long, desolate drive inland to Arcadia. Baking heat. Fear and embarrassment. That silence. Anger and dismay. And a rodeo. I seemed to recall being taken to a rodeo. Or maybe that was just a memory I created for a short story I once wrote about a young woman and her mentally ill mother. Any facts that may have remained had been obscured by my own fiction. What could I do? I studied the website photos, searching for something familiar.

About the first, I wondered: Had I ever walked through those front doors? Skinny arms wrapped around myself, to ward off the chill of the AC. It would've been very hot that time of year and I could easily have been wearing my favorite outfit, matching shorts and tank top the color of a Creamsicle. It would've been humid too. My mother's hair must've looked a fright. Did we all sit there in that brighter-than-imagined waiting room, flipping through outdated copies of "Golf Digest" or "Life" or "People"? Did I spend the time writing my novel? Did my sister sit and sulk in her new shoes, solving and resolving the Rubik's Cube?

In the second photo, could that have been the door where they took my mother? Had she hugged us goodbye? Given us a kiss? Did anyone tell us not to worry, everything was going to be OK? Of course not; that wasn't my grandparents' style. Nor my mother's, I don't think. The event would have played out as though it was the most natural in the world. No time for questions. The page had been turned. This was the story now.

Based on my nursing experience in psychiatric hospitals, I imagined the desk in the third photo was where the aides sorted through my mother's belongings, informing her of what she could keep with her—cosmetics, comb, clothes—though no belt or shoelaces. And what would be kept for her—pocketbook, cigarettes and lighter—though back then, who knows? Maybe the patients, doctors, nurses and staff all still smoked freely and everywhere. Could my mother hear people screaming and moaning down that long hallway? Was she scared? Did she know what was happening?

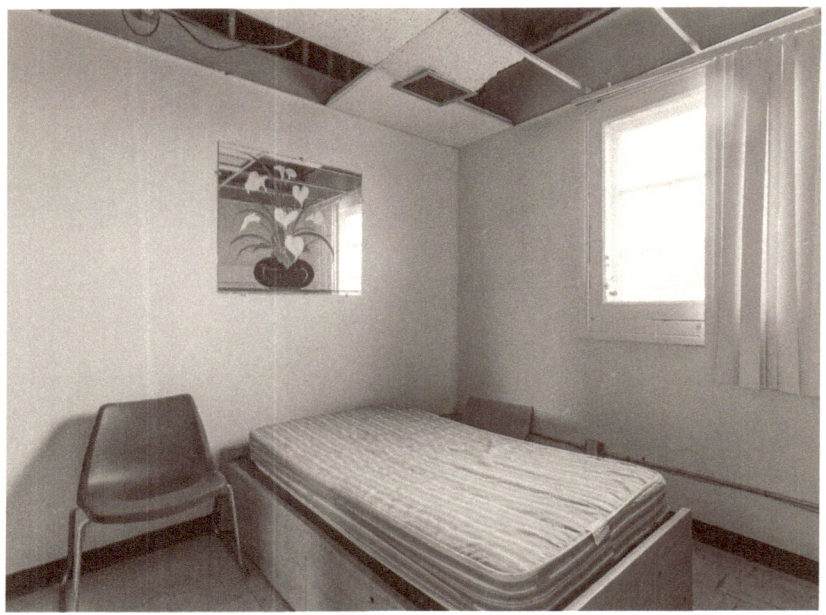

The fourth photo: How easily I could place my mother in that room. Sitting in that plastic chair, legs crossed, an open-toed wooden Dr. Scholl's dangling off her foot. Staring into space, a cigarette—she had to have a cigarette—burning between her fingers. I could see her at night, too, lying in that small bed with the overly bleached linens pulled up to her chin, thin blanket scratchy against her skin. Did she cry that first night? Ask to make a phone call? Finally, I could see her in the morning, looking out the window, at the sun rising as we believed it always would, wondering if she'd ever see her old life again.

Of all the photos I inspected, the last one was the only one familiar, and that was only because of a smell. It's said that scent bypasses the thalamus—an essential partner with the cortex in working memory—and goes straight to the olfactory bulb, which is directly connected to the amygdala, the seat of all emotions. The familiar smell that had haunted me for nearly 40 years was the root of the strong emotional memory I had of that place, specifically a bathroom in this place. The smell was a pungent commercial-grade cherry scent, which to me would forever smell like shock. Like loss. Like dread.

I was in high school when I learned the diagnosis my mother had been given at G. Pierce Wood: schizophrenia. A word unsoft as they come, with its short icky "i" and hissing "ts" sound. Up to that point, the only thing I knew about the disorder was from a jokey T-shirt: "I'm a schizophrenic and so am I." Like most people, I thought schizophrenia meant having a split personality. Like "Sybil" or "The Three Faces of Eve."

I wrote a paper about it for my 10th grade anatomy class, an encyclopedia my only reference as this was well before the Internet. Later, in my 40s, I inherited an old set after my sister-in-law died. I dug volume 20 (Collier's, 1962) out of the back of her music room closet: "The name applied to a group of mental diseases which are characterized fundamentally by severe disturbances in the thinking, feeling, and emotional contact of the individual with the outside world." Under the heading "Causation," the authors were as noncommittal as they would likely be today: "specific recessive genetic factors, pathological experiences in … early life, disturbances in glandular secretions, infections, injuries …"

For a long time, I believed it was sex that made my mother crazy—specifically, sex with Earl Brack. Sex was dark and scary to me, something I knew would one day be expected of me but that I was in no hurry to participate in. Not so my mother. My mother often boasted about her sexual escapades. I could picture her clearly at the kitchen table on Skyline Boulevard drinking her 90th cup of coffee and telling me how many men she'd slept with.

My mother loved men and men loved my mother. After Earl but before Tom, there was Skip the ex-con; Ron, another ex-con; Joe, who worked for the electrical company; Bobby, the sad divorcé; Jeff, who looked like Gene Wilder and always told dumb jokes; and Jon, the ex-race car driver with the fake hand. "She must take it up the ass," my first boyfriend once said. A crude truth, perhaps. My mother was earthy and bawdy. She kept raunchy porno mags unhidden on her bedside table. She liked to walk around naked and asked me mortifying questions. Once, riding in the car with her and Tom, she asked me, "Do you masturbate, Amy?" She was looking at Tom, who was driving, but talking to me. Tom replied almost on cue: "I don't masturbate Amy."

"I don't think your mother had schizophrenia," a psychiatric nurse colleague once said to me when I told her about my mother. "She sounds more manic." I balked at her comment: "That's what they told me! I wrote a paper on it in the 10th grade! That's what I've been telling myself for 30 years!"

I could see how my colleague would come to such a conclusion. My mother was very artistic and very sexual. Maybe she had schizoaffective disorder, bipolar type, which meant she had schizophrenia and bipolar disorder. That would explain the stony affect, the cold silences and bizarre comments, as well as the hypersexuality. But my mother was never manic in the clinical sense of the word. She was never a high-energy-on-little-sleep, grandiose, talk-a-mile-a-minute kind of gal. If anything, she was depressed. Slow and vacant and detached from the world. Unless men were involved.

Even with men, though, she would be distant. Even with her third husband, Tom—the man who supposedly could give her an orgasm with just a touch of his hand—she was often far away. Once in high school, I was out at their favorite diner with them. My mother sat and stared and smoked. When the food finally came, she continued to stare and smoke until Tom broke the silence. "That food's not gonna eat itself, Susan." My mother was slow to process but eventually smiled with one side of her mouth, crushed out her cigarette, and still staring, replied, "For sure."

My colleague's comments weren't the first that made me question my mother's diagnosis. Maybe I remembered everything wrong. Maybe I had just been dramatic all those years. Maybe there was something wrong with me.

But there were things I was certain happened. Like the Mad Lib incident in the trailer. My mother, before, may have been a vague character in my memory, but the woman who showed up in that bathroom long ago was distinctly there, and she was distinctly different.

And then these things too:

All the staring and smirking and nodding at nothing. Absolutely nothing;

Her telling me she heard tanks outside the trailer;

Her at the kitchen table at the duplex on Skyline when I was in high school, sitting in a way I could only describe as a swagger. It might have been Tom at the table with us or it could have been Skip, or one of the other boyfriends before or between them. Whoever it was, he and I ate while my mother chain-smoked and shook her leg. She took one of those indeterminately long drags on her cigarette and started to laugh. "I killed the goddamned man," she said, with that freaky glow in her one eye.

That's not mania. That's not depression. That's just fucking crazy.

And these things:

Coming home one day to find her on top of the dryer, scared and confused. Was this from being crazy or from being medicated for the last several years? I had no idea and would never know;

Her banging on my bedroom door early one morning demanding to know where the box was that held the axe so she could cut down the tree;

All the pacing and staring and not speaking or sleeping for literally days until my sister or I would make a desperate call to my father's brother, and he would bring over a six-pack of beer, even though it never took more than one to knock her out;

How during those episodes of pacing and staring and not speaking or sleeping for literally days I would scream in her face, and she would stare right past me, like neither of us were even there;

The multiple cigarettes burning in multiple ashtrays throughout the house, my sister or me crushing them all out and trying to hide her pack, only to have her suddenly come back to life asking where her cigarettes went;

The bottles of medications in the kitchen she hated to take. Thorazine first, then Stelazine. Later in life, Clozaril and Risperdal. All of them horrible, the shaking and shuffling of the older meds only to be replaced with the lethargy and weight gain of the newer ones.

Enough.

What was I trying to prove? And to whom? I didn't feel the same urgency I did when I was younger, but I was still searching for an answer. Why? Why did it happen and, more importantly, why did I care? I cared less once I was well past the age of developing the disorder. But the young girl who lost her mother was still around. Still waiting for an explanation that would satisfy.

Wanting or Willing

S ince I would never know why and how my mother's breakdown happened, I would have to be content with knowing the when and where. It happened in the trailer; that was fully established. The when was confirmed by way of the Edison Pageant of Light, my 10th birthday present from my sister, and a card I found that my father sent to my sister, dated May 10, 1982. These facts, cold and hard as they were, comforted me.

On the front of the card was a graphic of a tuxedo cat wearing a red tie embossed with a gold mouse. The cat's expression was sad and angry and annoyed all at once. Just like my sister usually looked. The cat was trying to save face with his spiffy tie but looked like he was losing the fight.

In the card, my father wrote: "I will talk to mom in a couple weeks when she is better about you and Amy coming up here for at least until next summer so she can have a chance to get back on her feet."

This surprised me. According to the story my sister and I had been telling ourselves for years, it was our grandmother who told my father he had to come get us. My sister and I had constructed whole scenes in our heads wherein we were abandoned, better off forgotten, wanted by no one. My father wanted us, though, apparently. Or at least he was willing to have us. What degree of difference was there between wanting and willing?

The card also demonstrated how naive my father was (how naive we all were) about my mother's breakdown. "A couple of weeks when she is better." None of us had any idea then what was really happening. We had not yet realized that the upheaval would result in an outright cleaving of past and future.

I showed the card to my sister in 2017 while we sat in her living room in the house she had bought with her share of our father's inheritance. I got the sense that the house was as close to a home as she'd ever felt she had. It was a home she earned by being a good daughter to a not-so-great parent. I handed the card to her, and she held it like it might bite. "Isn't that nice," she said, sounding sad and angry and annoyed all at once.

"It is," I said, suddenly feeling the need to defend him.

To me, it was a clue that he cared. My father had done something on his own to reach out to us, through my sister, no less. I was encouraged to learn of a time where he felt comfortable communicating with her, acknowledging her. I guess he had no choice then; I would've been too young to be the go-between.

I regretted not giving my father more credit. There was no way Nancy picked out this card for him, and that would normally have been her job, the buying of greeting cards. But this time my father surely made a special trip. I imagined him sneaking out of the office on his lunch break (he and Nancy both worked at IBM), going into a nearby drugstore, picking out this card special for my sister who loved cats, stashing the card in his briefcase, writing his note quickly but taking the time to write a P.S. ("Say Hi to Amy for me.") and a P.S.S. ("xoxoxoxoxoxo"). And right after "Love Always, Dad," a smiley face.

When our father came to Florida to pick us up in the summer of 1982, he didn't bother to tell us we would be going for the whole year. We thought we were just going on a trip for the summer. That was the way my sister and I continued to tell the story. A sad and tidy narrative to mirror what we had always believed about our first big trip, to Florida. The card I found from my father proved that he mentioned the possibility at least once. We couldn't really blame him, then, for the misunderstanding.

They came to fetch us in a car—my father, Nancy and Nancy's sister Sue. It was a typical sweltering Florida summer, and the air in the car was frosty. I caught a chest cold and spent much of the time curled up in the backseat, trying to take up as little space as possible, wincing every time I breathed.

My sister would have sat in the middle. Or would it have been Sue, there to keep my sister and me from bickering? No matter, my sister would have been angry. She had been for months. Angry at having to leave her friends, angry at suddenly having rules to follow, angry at Nancy and sister Sue for addressing her as Samantha while they had no problem calling me Amy. And she wouldn't have been quietly angry. She was sassy.

My father drove. I imagined he was, like me, trying to fade into the background. Not wanting to make the situation any worse than it already was. Nancy would have ridden in the front at his side, perpetually turned so she could keep an eye on him and us. I could imagine her periodically giving my father directives— "slow down," "don't pass," "watch that car"—tacking on "dear" each time in a tone that gave the word teeth.

He took us to Disney World on the way to Ohio (nowhere near on the way, now that I think about it), and we all strolled through the kingdom for the first time, hoping some of its magic might transform us.

No such alchemy occurred. Despite the few pictures snapped of my sister and me smiling as we should, I doubted we had any fun at all. We all left just as we had arrived.

My father's willingness to get us that summer was no small thing, I realized later. When it came to her husband's daughters, Nancy had proven herself jealous, unwavering in her resolve. I had no doubt she would have sent us into the woods to fend for ourselves had my mother not already done so when she left my father. Nancy lumped us in with my mother, as if we'd abandoned our father. "You had your chance," I could imagine her saying. "You've made your choice." She spent over 30 years marking her territory, protecting her borders, coveting my father for herself. How many times over the years had I called my father to say hello only to get an immediate call from Nancy afterward. "I heard you called Dad. What's up?"

To Nancy, our coming back to live with him had to have felt like an invasion. And even though my sister and I had nothing to do with that decision, Nancy treated our presence as a willful act of selfishness.

"She never forgave you two for coming to live with us that year your mom was sick," my father said to me years later, soon after Nancy died in 2013. The alcohol had once again loosened his tongue, and he confirmed what had been evident to me.

"We were just kids," I told him, exasperated, though in truth being a burden had always been something I felt I should apologize for.

The Shell Duck

B efore that awful car ride north—after the breaking down and the ensuing silence, but before the before and after—there was this:

At 10 years old, I was just a kid in the living room of my grandparents' condo in Cape Coral. It was dusk, right after dinner. The patio doors were open, and a breeze blew through the screen. In the air, the smell of mashed potatoes and canal water. I was sprawled on the floor, head propped on a throw pillow, trying to read a "Choose Your Own Adventure" book.

My mother—or at least someone resembling my mother—was home from the hospital. She sat in my grandfather's recliner, feet planted firmly on the carpet, hands gripping the arms of the chair, eyes squarely on me. My mother's expression for the moment was as flat as a forgotten glass of pop. Flat was better than some of her other recent expressions, like the one where her eyes squinted and she smiled, at nothing, with one side of her mouth.

I tried to focus on my book. Was it "The Abominable Snowman," the first volume, published in 1982? It would have had to be for this was the spring of 1982. What was it that I had to decide? To "make up a fantastic story (turn to page 59)" or "insist that I know nothing (turn to page 64)"?

Whatever the choice that evening, it would not have been easy to make, because no matter my mother's expression, she was lately almost always staring at me, or staring through me. I couldn't decide which was worse.

My grandmother, meanwhile, sat in the companion recliner, wearing her tan culottes and flip-flops. Her hands were soft and smelled like Nivea. I was terrified of her. She was usually yelling, but on this composite night of what must've been many nights in the spring of '82, she perched on the edge of her recliner, smiling, her teeth yellow-bluish like my mother's, from when she used to smoke. She stared at a decorative duck she'd found in a thrift shop and had placed in front of the television. It was made from shells and had googly eyes glued unevenly onto a large shell I would one day know is called a whelk. Its feet were huge orange clamshells, its body an even bigger whelk.

It stood about shin high and looked, at first glance, like I felt. Bewildered. As though it shared my fear and confusion at finding myself in the middle of an adventure I did not choose. One where my mother was no longer my mother, and my grandmother liked the orange shell duck more than any of us. More than my grandfather who was probably out for a walk. More than my sister who for some reason was nowhere in this memory. More than my mother. More than me.

I stared at the shell duck, and the shell duck stared back. Its expression, upon closer inspection, was kind and wise, as though it already knew all the possible outcomes to all the possible adventures. For the first time in months, I felt comforted, not quite safe and whole, but at least hopeful that I one day might again.

I have the shell duck still. It sits on my desk in my office where I regularly encourage the sad and confused, the grief-stricken and the lost, to see their situations in a different way. I always considered the shell duck's survival a marvel of circumstance, but then I think of all the times it has broken and all the times I've put it back together.

Four:

1982 to 1983, Ohio

Sorry

"Your mom is sick," my grandparents kept telling us. Sick seemed too simple a word to describe what had happened to my mother, but I didn't yet have the vocabulary to do any better. What was the word for when someone disappeared but was still there?

I knew other words, though: Fear. Hope. Loss. Guilt.

Fear was me watching "I Never Promised You a Rose Garden" on late-night TV when I was 10 or 11 and could not sleep. It was me whimpering with my arms around my knees because I didn't want to be locked up in a state hospital like my mother.

Hope was my father hearing me from upstairs and coming down to console me. It was me on his lap, what used to be my favorite place, expecting it to feel the same as it did when I was 3 eating Cool Whip out of the container. Soft and safe. Everything right with my world.

Loss was me being too big, my sleeves wet with snot. It was my father smelling stronger of Listerine than of the pipe tobacco I loved. It was our physical closeness seeming shameful and embarrassing. Loss asked, what had happened to us?

Guilt was the heavy mantle I gathered around me as I chanted "I'm sorry, I'm sorry, I'm sorry" between hiccups and heaves. As though words alone could mend us.

Words Alone

I could not seem to find a single photograph from that year my sister and I spent with my father and Nancy. How was that possible? Were we all so miserable none of us wanted any proof that the year had occurred? Were we all hoping to wake up the following spring, as if from a bad dream, and pretend nothing ever happened? I wouldn't doubt it. Inept as we'd been in many ways, my family had always been skilled at ignoring crucial pieces to our shared story.

Good thing my memories from this era were some-what intact.

The house or townhouse, like every house I've lived in, I remembered well. It was part of a community called Bunting Tree. The sign at the entrance had a bird on it, and of course, a tree.

I didn't need a satellite view to recall the neighborhood layout, but I looked it up anyway, first searching the county recorder's office website for the original deed to get the address.

Surprisingly, the condo was for sale, and photos were posted online. The inside looked a little shabby, with its plain walls and tired-looking carpet, so different from the stylishness I recalled. But I had come from a double-wide trailer with rats and ants, so I could understand why a middle-class condo in a Cleveland suburb looked fancy to me. The condo had three bedrooms and two and a half baths. And when my father and Nancy lived there, a full basement complete with a well-stocked bar, pool table, beer can collection lining the walls, and, in a separate basement room, my father's stained glass workshop.

The basement was my favorite place in the townhouse, for it held most of the furniture I remembered from the house where my father, my mother, my sister and I all lived together. The rocking chair with the wine-colored cushion, one of the side tables with the puzzle top my father and mother had made together when they were married. It seemed everything from my father's pre-Nancy life was relegated to the basement. Only his stereo system with the reel-to-reel was allowed in the living room. Nancy had no knowledge, apparently, of how my father once listened to "Fire and Rain" pondering the fate of his first wife and second daughter.

The main floor comprised the dining area, living room, kitchen and half bath, which itself was bigger than both the trailer bathrooms combined. Upstairs, three bedrooms, two full baths. The color scheme throughout the condo was muted earth tones. The only splash of color I recalled was the dark blue floral wallpaper in my sister's room. The color was so dark it seemed to press in, well past the comfort of an embrace. My room, by contrast, was light, filled with new things that weren't mine and never would be.

Outside, in the back, was a patch of woods I'd walk through to get to the mailbox I'd check every day for letters from

Heather or my mother. I loved getting letters, although seeing my mother's shaky handwriting always made me feel sad and squirrely. Still, the letters gave me a sense of being connected to the place I considered home.

There were many kids in the neighborhood, and if I had lived there longer, I no doubt would have come to know their names. Like the kids in Maple Heights and River Trails, they played the familiar yard games, only these North Royalton kids usually played in the woods after dark, something I was too scared to consider doing even if I hadn't been so shy.

Many of the kids rode their bikes and skateboards down the long, steep main road, Washington Avenue. I envied their courage, in particular one girl whose name I once knew but had long forgotten. She was blonde, boyish and bold looking, a young Jodie Foster, somewhere in age between my sister and me, always out in the middle of the group, appearing so sure, so at home. I may have only met her once, or maybe I saw her often. Either way, I thought of her a lot during that year. She seemed to me the kind of girl I might have been, would have liked to have become, had a different adventure been chosen for me.

My father and Nancy tried their best to go on about their lives as before—before they had two kids to worry about. And my sister and I tried our best to go on about ours—before we had two parents to worry about.

Though my father and Nancy definitely had more rules for us to follow than my mother (a curfew, for instance, and a bedtime), my sister and I still had a lot of time to ourselves. My father and Nancy both worked at IBM, usually until 5 or 6 p.m. My sister, preferring to spend her time with anyone other than her little sister, was often gone as well, leaving me alone most afternoons.

I spent much of that time writing poetry, carefully printing my just-as-carefully metered rhymes in a journal my grandmother had bought for me before we were taken north. The hard-bound journal had a glossy light purple cover and lined pages. I had been writing poetry since the first grade, simple verses about simple things, like love and hearts. But my poetry changed once we moved, becoming more serious with the sadness I was beginning to carry. Part of me liked how mature the melancholy made me feel. I was growing up, becoming aware that there was a life ahead of me and behind me, not just in front of and around me. How I wished I'd found that journal of fifth grade poetry. What else might those poems tell me about who I was then, what life was like for me?

I also spent a lot of time snooping. I loved looking through Nancy's jewelry box. The lining of the box smelled of her perfume, a floral-like scent as sharp as it was sweet. Unlike my mother, who preferred silver and turquoise, Nancy was partial to gold and diamonds. She had a collection of pins, including one of a simple gold "N" my sister and I had picked out for her at Kmart one year for her birthday. Another of a gold teddy bear— she loved teddy bears. I'd hold the gold pieces in my hands, each one flashing in the dim afternoon light filtering in through the windows. There was a white ceramic heart pendant I was especially fond of. It had heft and smoothness, just like sadness.

In their bedside tables were stacks of "Playboy." I'd sit on their bed listening to the top hits of the early '80s on the clock radio and look through the magazines. Such a nostalgic sound, that early '80s soft rock, with none of the flash of disco that came before it and none of the fluff of the post-Madonna pop yet to come. I liked the soft stuff: Juice Newton and Air Supply; Stevie Nicks and Neil Diamond. My mother's influence, no doubt. But I also liked things she hated: Steve Miller and Men at Work; J. Geils and Joan Jett. I was at the age where I started to listen to the words as much as to the melody. Singing along under my breath, I'd flip to the centerfold and read the biographical material, always amazed at how pretty the handwriting was. And the girls, of course. So flawless.

In their bathroom, I'd examine all of Nancy's cosmetics. The various shades of pink lipsticks, eyeliner pencils and eyeshadow kits. Lots of Clinique and Lancôme and Estée Lauder; brands you wouldn't find at Kmart. She had an old-fashioned comb, brush and mirror set of gold filigree. With my back to the bathroom mirror, I'd hold the small mirror up in front of me and think I didn't look half bad from the back. My hair was long and wavy thanks to a perm someone had given me. From the front, though, I looked a mess. My bangs were crooked and short thanks to a haircut by my sister. And my nose—could it have been any bigger?

On my father's side was a bottle of Listerine, various aftershaves, and a funny hair dryer that looked like a brush. My father was as fastidious about his appearance as Nancy was about hers. Many mornings I'd perch on their bed and watch them both preen.

One morning, I asked them if I could read a poem I had written. I recited the first two lines: "The world is the rain and I am its seedling. Trying to grow but never succeeding."

My father, putting the final touches to his hair, looked at my reflection in the mirror. "That's lovely, dear."

"Thom," Nancy said, slipping on her flats. "We'll be late."

I was the last to leave in the morning and the first to come home in the afternoon. The mornings were scarier. Maybe because I was the one left in the house. It was different after school when I was the first one to come home. The fear resided in the being left behind, not so much the being alone. I'd go to the bus stop early. Sometimes by an hour. I had done this in the trailer too, but that was motivated by a fear of being late. Even outside of the empty townhouse, there were fears. What if I got on the wrong bus? What if it took me somewhere far away? What if it never brought me back? As I waited for other kids to get there, I'd sit on the Bunting Tree sign, my feet dangling, seemingly carefree, tennis shoes scuffing against the wood, while fear curled heavy in my lap, like a cat.

I liked school, as I had always liked school. I made what you might call friends easier than I thought I would. My teacher's husband worked for IBM like my father did. "You've been moved!" she said to me when we met and my father told her I was from Florida. She was playing on the common joke among the company's employees who were used to being moved around for work. I liked her. She seemed to understand the things that were beginning to matter to me.

When she gave us an assignment to make a list of "soft words," I felt like she had opened a door and invited me inside. I wrote the words carefully on my paper, one after the other, like a string of pearls. Lullaby, hush, whisper, soothe. Each one light yet rich, each one an antidote to sadness. My teacher gave me an A, and when the teacher-parent open house came along, she told my father I was a bright child.

I joined band and chose the cornet. My father teased me, calling me Doc Severinsen after the guy who played on the Johnny Carson show. I practiced dutifully, but I was terrible. I couldn't figure out how to read the music, and I was too afraid to ask for help. The night of the big concert, I locked myself in a bathroom stall and refused to come out. My father was kind and came to fetch me, telling me through the door that I didn't have to play if I didn't want to.

All my girlfriends stayed in band after I quit, so one day a week, I'd go out for recess without them. One day, a group of boys from my class jumped me on the playground. I didn't remember much of the incident. I was held down. They were laughing. Dirt and grass might've been shoved into my mouth. I was certainly crying. They let me go when the whistle blew.

Back in class, I hiccuped with rage. I took out a piece of paper and wrote a new list of words. Cocksucker, son of a bitch, motherfucker, asshole. These were hard words picked up from my sister's friends and my mother's boyfriends. No one in my family swore like that. With shaking hands, I folded the paper and passed it to the ringleader, a short boy with dark hair and a bright smile. He opened the note, then, smiling his bright smile, walked up to the teacher and gave it to her. I bolted from the room and locked myself in that same bathroom stall. Like my father, my teacher was kind and said all the right words to coax me out.

I hadn't often thought about how my father must have felt during our year with him. In the years that followed, it was easier to gloss over the messy nuances of experience and adopt yet another categorical pronouncement: They never wanted us there. And as he would later tell me himself: his lifestyle really didn't have room for two kids; Nancy resented us being there; et cetera.

Yet my father was a good guy overall, and we were his girls. I liked to think that his willingness to care for us that year went beyond just obligation. I liked to think he welcomed our presence as a second chance to make things right, even if just for a year.

Memories of mine and my sister's seemed to speak to his wanting to be a father again. He bought us an Atari game system, for instance, and arranged for horseback riding lessons. He welcomed our friends over (I had one best friend, Sherry; my sister, a girl named Chris), and he took us out to eat often at the putt-putt pizza place up the road. He helped my sister hone her pool-playing skills and provided me with reams of computer paper from his job at IBM for me to color on. He didn't work on stained glass with us much that year that I remember, but at least on one night when I couldn't sleep and was upset and crying, he tried his best to comfort me. And for that Christmas, he went behind Nancy's back and bought my sister a Puma T-shirt she wanted.

"She was so pissed," my sister told me.

"Over a T-shirt?" I asked.

My sister made a face of mock seriousness. "It wasn't what they had agreed upon."

We weren't what they had agreed upon, either, and us being there almost cost him his second marriage. At some point during that year, I became aware that Nancy had threatened to leave. While I didn't have a great fondness for her, I hated the thought of them being unhappy because of me. I knew, even before my father told me so many years later, that any conflict in their marriage was our fault. The morning after what must've been a huge fight—perhaps the fight where Nancy threatened to leave—I wrote her a note, apologizing for everything, begging her not to go. I wanted us to be a family, I told her. I wanted everything to work out.

When she found it, she hugged me close and cried, "Oh, Amy. I love you too." Then she kissed me on the cheek and rubbed at the pink stain left behind—rubbing it off or in, who could tell.

I never considered what that year must have been like for my mother, either. It seemed I was starting to compartmentalize around this time, perhaps to cope with the changes, the sadness, the fear. These pieces go here; those there. Forget trying to see a big picture. Just focus on what's in front of you. Or maybe, I was still merely taking her for granted. Although I received many letters from her, I couldn't recall what the letters said. Surely, she wrote that she missed us. That she loved us. That she couldn't wait until we could come home. And my sister and I would have written back the same. Did we ever talk to her on the phone? We must have. A year is too long a time not to make a phone call. What did we talk about? Did I call her mom or mommy? Was she sad after she hung up? Was I? Once again, when it came to my mother and me, back then, I remembered so little. Every time I tried to find her, I lost her all over again.

How much did I share with her about my new albeit temporary life? I doubted I told her about Jason N. Though I still pined—would always pine—for the mythologized Matt Martell, Jason was my crush in the fifth grade. He and I never spoke. He had no idea who I was. I didn't recall how I knew who he was;

he was in another class. He wasn't much of a babe, as we said in those days. In fact, I thought he looked like the number six. I looked at his picture in my Royal View School yearbook. He still looked like the number six. Something in the roundness of his face, the soft contour of his teeth. Though I was pretty sure he had no knowledge of my love for him, my school friends did. Several autographs in my yearbook were from girls wishing me "Good luck with the boys and with Jason."

My friend Sherry—at the time, the only girl I considered a real friend and not just an acquaintance—was sweet on a boy named Scott. Jason and Scott were best friends. Sherry and I were best friends. It seemed fated that we girls should be with those boys. But the only place we were ever with them was in our dreams. On those reams of paper my father brought home from IBM for me to color on, Sherry and I wrote out our fantasies. They usually began with: Sherry and Amy are walking to the store where they meet Jason and Scott behind the building. In some versions, Scott French-kisses Sherry, and Jason Frenches Amy. In others, one of us gives one of them a blowjob. In still others, we all have sex and make babies and get married and live happily ever after. We'd draw big smiley faces with feet, arms and antennae. We'd draw hearts with our initials inside and tiny arrows piercing through the centers. An apt image of the pain of unrequited love. That's how we spent our time, in the basement, crayons in hand, giggling over things we thought we understood.

Turned out I was wrong. There were photographs from this era. Plenty, in fact. During the process of writing about the time, the pictures materialized in my memory as clearly as if I held them in my hands.

Several were taken at Christmastime, including one of my father and me in front of the tree. My memory wanted me to believe I was wearing thick glasses with pale plastic frames that made me look like John Denver. But I wouldn't have those glasses until the sixth grade. I knew there was one of me and my father and my sister. His arm was around both of us, holding us close with just a hint of awkwardness. My father and I looked straight at the camera, but my sister bowed her head, still hating to be photographed. My favorite, though, the one I really couldn't believe I forgot, was of my father and Nancy. She was in the background clearing off an end table in the living room while my father sat in the chair, glancing at the camera, picking his nose. I loved the simple familiarity of that picture. I had always loved it. When I was younger—middle school, high school—I'd stare at it and let myself believe that at some point the "second" four of us were once, momentarily, if not happy, at least comfortable with each other.

What did it mean, my lapse of memory? What did it say about me to assume we all wanted to forget that year ever happened? Perhaps it belied the deep-rooted tendency we all have to toss aside the pieces of our story that seem too much a bother. The pieces that were jagged and ugly or simply just complicated the picture we'd tried to create, or the one we'd tried to sustain.

I eventually found those pictures from the year my sister and I lived with our father and Nancy. They were in a multi-photo frame of light oak; one of two such frames I had put together in my 30s and presented to my father for his birthday in a feeble stab at sentimentality. My own attempt to hold onto something we probably never had. After Nancy died, and my sister and I went through her things, we found both frames squirreled away in her closet, buried beneath Franklin Covey planner inserts and other high-end stationery supplies. Further proof in my mind we weren't wanted.

We weren't wanted. I was still trying to wrap up the story with that sad and tidy bow. The messy truth was, it was a raw and complicated time we all would have liked to forget. Forget my sister and Nancy fighting over who got the most attention from one of my father's young, handsome friends; over how much milk and butter to put in Kraft macaroni and cheese; over my sister playing music too loud and leaving hair in the sink. Forget my parents dragging us to parties because they didn't have a sitter, then dumping us into someone's living room to sleep on the floor while they sat in the other room drinking and laughing and trying to forget they had children in their charge. Forget the constant feelings of intrusion and inconvenience, unwantedness and loneliness.

But if I forgot all those things, I wouldn't remember the good things. The times when I did feel we were wanted and loved, like we belonged. Like the many photographs I found of my sister and her cat Spooky sitting on my father's and Nancy's bed doing her homework or wrapping Christmas presents. What a familiar, intimate scene: a child sitting on her parents' bed performing normal acts of childhood. Or like getting dressed up to dine at the fancy Japanese steakhouse or the even fancier Brown Derby. Or like finding the gold "N" pin in Nancy's jewelry box. Why would she keep something she must've found cheap and beneath her if somewhere in her cold, hard heart there wasn't a small soft place for us? Or like getting to see my father every day and feeling his arm around me, his hand giving my shoulder a squeeze, saying "Hello, Amo" as he puffed on his pipe.

In my mind, I conjured a picture of myself during this year. Of me sitting at my father's basement bar, skinny ankles poking out my high water jeans, 7Up in a fancy glass, a maraschino cherry sweet on my tongue, feeling grown-up and special, and, at least for a moment, like I was right where I was supposed to be.

Five:

1983 to 1985, Florida

Solace

I was 12 years old, maybe 13, sitting between Doug and Kevin in Doug's 1977 Chevy Malibu Classic. They were high school boys, hand-me-down friends of my sister's. We were parked in a vacant lot next to Doug's house, drinking beer one of them had scored from his older brother. I hated the taste of the beer, but I drank it anyway; I liked how it heightened my precocious teenage angst.

My mother was the reason for my angst. My crazy mother. I didn't know her actual diagnosis yet. I just knew she was fucking weird and sometimes scary, and no one else I knew had a parent like her.

In Doug's Malibu, sitting between those two boys, I got drunk and cried about how my mother was fucking weird and often scary and how I was so afraid and lonely sometimes I didn't know what to do. I cried so hard I could barely breathe. My head throbbed as I heaved and hiccuped. But it felt good to let it out. I was used to crying alone in my room, silently so no one could hear, though there was never anyone to hear.

I leaned into Doug's shoulder and made a mess of his shirt with the gobs of snot coming out of my nose. His shirt was unbuttoned. His chest was smooth. And even through my stuffed-up nose I could smell the strong, rich scent of boy sweat and beer.

What did they say, those young boys, to that even younger girl seeking solace? I couldn't recall. They simply sat there with me while I cried, their presence a comfort I had not felt since I was a little girl nestled in my father's warm lap.

The Returning

I couldn't say I wished we had stayed with my father and Nancy longer than a year, but I wouldn't have minded. I had adapted, as was my nature. My sister, though, was adamant. And years later, she was still adamant. "There was no way in hell I was going to stay with them." It had been a rough year, with my sister and Nancy constantly fighting, my father and I constantly placating. I imagined everyone was relieved when my sister decided we were going home.

Home wasn't the same. My mother was remarried by the time we got back and living with her second husband in a duplex near the police station in Cape Coral, a city of obsessively gridded streets, over 400 miles of man-made canals, and strategically planted palm trees. When developers came in the late '50s, the land was a vast morass. Within a remarkably short period of time, the wetlands were drained, the grid laid, the concrete poured. Though I didn't know any of this then, I could sense the rootlessness. Nothing belonged here in this artificial city, including me. This new home was home in name alone.

Surely in one of the letters from my mother that I couldn't recall she must've mentioned getting married again, but it wouldn't have mattered if I hadn't known. Surprises didn't bother me so much anymore. In fact, I found myself facing the question "What's next?" more with anticipation than dread, more curiosity than bewilderment. Perhaps this started even before we were sent north. When we lived briefly at my grandparents' condo there in that artificial city, before our year in Ohio, I'd stand on the landing outside their second story front door, my hands gripping the wrought iron "W" of the Windsor Manor logo, and pretend I was at the helm of some great ship, captain of my own destiny. Though even then, or by then, I was aware of the tempering, steering forces of wind and wave.

I spent many of those initial hot and humid days alone in front of the television in the duplex, the living room dark and cold, watching movies on HBO. "Poltergeist." "Author! Author!" "Grease 2." Disappearing children, unwanted children, children playing grown-up and looking for love. Those movies seemed to encapsulate elements of my young life thus far. I watched those movies again and again, sometimes twice in one day. There was solace to be found in getting repetitively lost in other peoples' stories. And the cold dark of the overly-air-conditioned apartment was a shelter from the overly bright, stark and baking streets.

I must have met my mother's second husband, Hank, before he became my first stepfather. He was the son of my mother's preacher at the Science of Mind Center. He was a former trucker, and though I didn't remember where he worked when he was with us, it was something blue collar. My mother only dated blue collar men. Like Earl Brack, Hank had his name stitched in white letters on his shirt. He had red hair and a matching mustache and smelled like burritos. I don't think my mother loved Hank so much as needed someone to take care of her. She would've been fresh out of the state mental hospital in August of 1982 when they married.

My mother never spoke much about her experience in the hospital. Her breakdown and illness went unacknowledged even when it was conspicuous. Everyone knew it had happened— was happening during the times her symptoms reemerged—but nobody spoke about it. Even my sister and I never spoke about it until much later, in our 20s, mainly to ask each other, "Did this really happen? Did we make it all up?" Of course, we hadn't made it up. My mother once bragged about the psychiatrist in Arcadia being impressed that she could correctly complete a newspaper crossword puzzle in ink. And once, crying, she mentioned the shock treatments.

In the summer of '83, though, she seemed back to normal. No staring or saying scary things; that would come again later. She got up every day and went to work, at a print shop, I was sure. Other than a brief stint at a restaurant called Grandma's

Chicken in the late '80s, my mother always worked at print shops. We spent Sundays at the center, which I loved because we got to sing and draw, and there was that optimistic view they offered of every one of us being co-creators of our own lives— lives filled with possibility and meaning. Later we'd go to dinner at Hank's parents' house for spicy Mexican food. My mother laughed often at Hank's dumb jokes, played the piano, and even enrolled my sister and me in school.

I was surprised to discover that my mother had been capable of such a routine parental task post-breakdown. In the dominating narrative of what was left of my childhood post-breakdown, my sister and I were abandoned, neglected, left to our own devices. "We didn't really have parents," my sister told her youngest son when I was telling him a story about when I was his age. A letter I found in a random envelope in my father's basement after his death proved how wrong I'd been.

Fri, June 24

Dear Mom:

Just a note to let you know the girls are doing fine. They are at my folks tonite. Mom & Dad enjoy them — Chris, too. Thank & I think she's a great young woman. The girls want to go to the beach on Sunday. So far, I think we'll make it!

Chris told me she plans on flying back July 4th — leaving here @ 11:45 that Monday. I'll see she phones up north before she leaves.

I have a few needs before school opens + a question or two.

Before the 15th of July, I need from you what the School Board calls a "Supervisory Care Form" — filled out by you + notarized — apparently a notary can give you this form. It shows you have custody and that you're agreed to leave them with me

Susan Douglas

(over)

171

- 2 -

for this school year. Perhaps
your School Board can point
you in the right direction.

I also need the addresses &
phone #'s of their schools &
their doctor in No. Regatton.
I need a copy of their physical
the doctor gave them within
one year ago & a copy of their
shot (immunization) records. If
you can't come up with these
please notify me because I'd
have a _lot_ of back-tracking
to do down here with Dr. O'Brian.
I'd have to set up a physical
before July 20th, too!

Once I get all this from
you, I'll register them before
Aug. 10th — I have birth certificates
with me.

I figured the first support
check comes for July and so-on
on or around the end of the
month. It used to be around
the 28th of ea. month. It helps
me to avoid the rush of
social security folks at the end
of the month.

The girls did a remarkable

- 3 -

Susan Douglas

job of organizing their room. Even with Chris, it's not as crowded as I'd imagined it might be.

Well, I've gotta' close.

It was very nice to see Myke again, after 5 or 6 years! And thanks again for all your help.

Give my best to Nancy & to your folks.

Love,
Susan

Physical Exam Records
Immunization Records
School Records

ALBAN MIDDLE SCHOOL

237-8800

The letter stunned me when I first read it in my father's basement in 2015, crouched among the many bags and boxes containing the remnants of his 68 years of life. I was stunned by the sheer normality of its content. "Look at this," I had told my sister, handing over the sheets of paper as though they held some shocking secret.

My mother wrote the letter on her personal stationery, with her new name below a graphic of what could be considered an avatar today. It was dated Friday, Jun. 24, and began with "Dear Thom" and a colon. She knew him well enough by then to include the "h" in his name, but her use of a colon instead of a comma hinted at a certain formality. The tone of the letter was direct with just enough chattiness to solidify something I remembered clearly about the two of them, together, after the divorce at least—they were always cordial with one another.

The letter showed a responsible, conscientious mother trying to gather the necessary documents to enroll her children in a new school district. She wrote about a supervisory care form that my father, who apparently had custody of us then (I didn't know that), needed to sign and have notarized, thus granting my mother the authority to keep us in her charge for the school year. (At what point and by what manner my mother regained legal custody of us would remain unknown to me. I tried finding information via the Cuyahoga and Lee County clerk of courts Internet case search to no avail.) My mother was clear about when she needed this form—"before the 15th of July"—and she even suggested that he might find guidance with his local school board. My mother's soft skills really shone there. Despite her penchant for bohemianism and blue collar men, she hadn't forgotten her middle-class roots.

She then requested the addresses and phone numbers of our schools and doctor, as well as our immunization records. She asked my father to please let her know if he couldn't come up with the records because she'd have "a lot of back-tracking to do … with Dr. O'Brian." I was stunned when I read those lines. We had a doctor? The only doctors I remembered going to post-breakdown were the ones who worked at the free clinic in Fort Myers, a place I went to only with my sister. A place filled with hookers and junkies and stray kids like us. Realizing my mother may have taken us to a doctor was the equivalent of realizing how many miles my father drove for us when we were little. Astounding.

After some talk about the support check they must have discussed outside of the letter, my mother resumed the chattiness and even sent her best to Nancy and his folks. She ended with "Love, Susan" and her signature star, which was her self-proclaimed nickname.

I couldn't help noticing that I sign the "A" in my name with a similar flourish as my mother's "S." And I would have made a similar list of items needed, just as my father noted on the letter.

We lived for a bit in that duplex near the police station, then moved to a three-bedroom house on Southeast 30th Street in a well-established middle class neighborhood of similar stucco ranch homes off Del Prado Boulevard—an important distinction. Having consulted an online map, I learned the streets in that artificial city were so obsessively gridded, that our Southeast 30th Street followed a longitudinal line westward, continuing even when interrupted by canals and latitudinal side streets, which meant there were Southeast 30th Streets off Academy and Santa Barbara Boulevards, too. It was the same for all the numbered streets and avenues, terraces, places and lanes. Each section of each same-named road stretched out, cut off, alone.

I remembered this house perhaps best of all, but when I looked it up online, my certainty faltered. It was listed as a four-bedroom, three-bath home. I was sure it only had three and two. The photo of the house was familiar enough. The garage was on the left side, there was an octagon window where my mother's bathroom was, and there was the triple front window in the living room. Still, there had been changes over the last several decades. The front stoop was enclosed, the yard was fenced in, and there was a circular driveway and professional landscaping. The satellite view even showed there was a pool. Was this really my old house? I dug a little deeper. With the parcel number I searched for any permits that may have been granted after 1984 to add on that bed and bathroom. I found nothing. As far as the county officials were concerned, this house on Southeast 30th Street was built with four bedrooms and three baths.

I was just about to panic—was everything I thought I knew wrong?—when I found confirmation of my mother's and Hank's marriage settlement agreement from March of 1984, which I was able to view on the Lee County Clerk of Courts website:

"The premises is a three-bedroom two-bath home ..." Who knew when and how those two extra rooms were added. I was just relieved to know there were places where my memory did not fail me.

My mother's second marriage was short; just under two years. According to that marriage settlement, my mother and Hank rented the big house on Southeast 30th Street in August 1983 and the lease was up in July 1984. Hank left much sooner, though exactly when I could not say. I assumed by March when they signed the settlement. At first, I misread the settlement and understood it to say that we moved out of the house on Southeast 30th Street in July 1984. After a recount of the months on my fingers, I gleaned our time there to be just 12 months. Impossible. So much happened in that house, time stretched so long—in the best way—in that house. How could it have only been a year? Upon further investigation consulting mainly my middle school yearbooks, I determined that we lived in that house for almost two years, moving out sometime in early 1985.

That made a little more sense. But still. Just under two years?

One of my writing mentors used to teach that there were two different kinds of time: Kronos, chronological time, the methodical tick-tick-tick-of-a-clock time, mundane time, forgettable time; and Kairos, emotional time, meaningful time, rich and unhurried time. Two eras of my life stretched out in that way: the first three years of college and those nearly two years on Southeast 30th Street. I had an actual photo album of my time in college, one I could flip through at my leisure and relive some of those fond moments. For the time on Southeast 30th Street, since there were so few photos to revisit, I'd have to compile an imaginary photo album, one consisting of the many mental pictures—some sweet, some bitter—that illustrated that first best time of my life.

Snapshots: Southeast 30th Street

MY ROOM

Near the front of the house, just off the family room, was my room. There was the round, green tweed couch someone had given us for me to sleep on. There was the milk crate on which I set my turntable. Eventually, someone would give me a mattress with a box spring, and I'd buy a headboard with a $20 bill I found in a field under a Zippo lighter near the police station. The headboard would have a shelf with small sliding doors. My mother would buy me an alarm clock, one of those old-fashioned ones with the double bells. None of it would be much, but it would be mine.

RECORD COLLECTION

Thanks to Columbia House's 10-for-a-penny sale, I would, over those two years, grow my record collection: Scorpions, Billy Squier, Michael Jackson, The Doors, Foreigner, Loverboy, The Who, Queen, Men At Work. Pink Floyd. I would also grow my mother's debt when I didn't think to cancel the membership.

THE FAMILY ROOM

Just outside my room was the family room. There was the couch with the geometric pattern in tan, black and orange. The material was smooth and cool on your skin. Not long after moving into the house, Hank would sleep on that couch, and once he moved out, Jon K., a friend of my mother's from the coffee shop, would sleep there. The tables at each end of the couch were dark, heavy octagons with doors that swung open. It was in there we kept the photo albums with their pictures of seemingly happier days. Right next to my bedroom door was the rattan rocker where my mother sat most evenings eating Doritos out of the bag. Sometimes, if she'd already taken her medication, the chips would miss her mouth and land in her lap. We had a color television on a stand. That's where you'd find me most afternoons after school, sprawled on the floor in front of it, my head propped on a couch pillow, my hand in the same bag of Doritos, watching whatever the television had to offer: "Three's Company," "M*A*S*H," "Laverne and Shirley," "Alice." I always laughed out loud. There was no one to disturb.

THE PATIO

Large, empty and screened in, the patio overlooked the backyard, which was a perpetually brown stretch of coarse grass about as inviting as a cactus. Before my sister introduced me to all of her friends and they—like everything else of hers—became mine, I'd spend my time alone, like I always had. You could find me those first few weeks out on the patio sitting at a box draped with a towel that I used as a table, listening to Top 40 radio or writing poetry. On at least one day, I made a list in a notebook of every song played and wondered why I bothered even as I did it. It was lonely those first few weeks. Time dragged so slowly. The fear I had in the trailer of being disappeared in the night started to haunt me during the long, quiet days. Being on the patio helped. It was almost outside, and I could see that the world was still there, ugly and stark as it was.

SMOKING

On the back patio, I smoked my first cigarette, one of my mother's Camel Light 100 stubs. I smoked to ward off the fear of ceasing to exist. I coughed and coughed and almost threw up. Still, when I'd smoked it down to the butt, I got another from one of my mother's many ashtrays.

THE LIVING ROOM

The biggest room in the house had three large front windows with curtains rarely drawn. It had my mother's piano, a metal shelving unit, a stereo. That was all. When Heather spent the night, we'd spread the king-sized quilt my great-grandmother made and sleep on the floor.

THE DOORS

I listened to The Doors for the first time in the living room, on a cassette tape my father made for me of their debut self-titled album. Why he thought I'd like them, I didn't know (I don't think he liked them), but there I was, bobbing my head to the opening bossa nova drum groove (thank you, Wikipedia) of "Break on

Through" and feeling immediately that this music was mine. I turned the volume up and danced with the dust motes near the front windows, my skinny legs and hips awkward as I tried to find some kind of rhythm. By the beginning of "The End," I may have been crying. Jim Morrison's lyrics conjured anticipation; they conjured sorrow. There was a filling up, an emptying out.

SOUL KITCHEN
Once I started smoking regularly, I would act out "Soul Kitchen" for my audience of none. I would light another cigarette. I would learn to forget.

MY MOTHER'S ROOM
On the other side of the house from my room, beyond the kitchen, just off the furnished but infrequently used dining room, was my mother's room. It was completely furnished with a matching bedroom set, a gift from her second set of in-laws. The room was dark and cool, with overflowing ashtrays on the bedside table, dresser and bathroom counter. The sheets were rumpled; they smelled of smoke and sweat.

MY MOTHER'S CLOSET
I moved through the folds of my mother's clothes in her walk-in closet. Silky dresses in earth and pastel tones, denim skirts, cotton tops. The softness enveloped me as I breathed in the various smells of her. Sand and Sable, Jovan Musk, Camel Lights. I slipped my feet into her clunky Dr. Scholl's sandals,

her knee-high moccasin boots, and pretended that we were still what we used to be, though even then, I could not remember what that was.

SMURF FOLDERS

My mother brought a set of school folders home to me before the start of sixth grade. On the covers, Papa Smurf and Smurfette, probably Brainy too. They were atrocious and I hated them, with their primary colors and glossy sheen. They were so fourth grade. So pre-breakdown. Didn't my mother know I was not a kid anymore? I smoked cigarettes. I listened to The Doors. I used college-ruled paper and preferred colors of a more somber tone. I cried over those stupid folders. I was young and melodramatic, believing that those innocuous school supplies were confirmation of some grave, irrevocable loss.

MY SISTER'S ROOM

Down a small hallway from the family room was my sister's room. She had a mattress sans box spring against one wall, and a long oak dresser against another. On the walls were posters of kittens, mostly bought at school book fairs. There was a stained glass mirror our father made her. Eventually there was a poster of Jim Morrison on the back of the door and a black light to make it glow. Next to the bed was a homemade wood box upon which our friends would scrawl graffiti. Someone would write "Fuck Athority" (sic) on it before the two years were out.

MY SISTER AND HER FUTURE FIRST HUSBAND
Before they moved out or got kicked out, my sister and her future first husband locked themselves in my sister's room for hours at a time, the Scorpions or Bob Seger blaring from behind the cheap, hollow door. They'd stumble out periodically, reeking of sex and weed, staying out just long enough to make cheese omelets or raid the freezer for Pudding Pops.

FITS
I threw fits. Over my sister yelling at me for wearing her clothes. Over my sister locking me out of the bathroom. Over my sister and her future first husband eating all of the Pudding Pops. When I threw fits, I liked to kick things. I made holes with my foot in our cheap, hollow doors.

MY SISTER'S BEDROOM WINDOW
Our friends crawled through my sister's bedroom window to hang out and party. That is, until we realized they could simply walk through the front door.

MY MOTHER'S FREAK-OUTS
That's what my sister and I called our mother's episodes: freak-outs. Maybe because they freaked us out. She did not go to work. She paced the house in silence, chain-smoking and looking through us as though we were not there. Sometimes, she'd go to take a drag on her cigarette and her hand would stop in mid-air, frozen in time and space, smoke curling around her fingers. My mother's illness was as quiet as smoke. A thick and stifling

airless quiet. The quiet of nothingness. Canned laughter on the television helped. The crunch of Doritos. The Doors on the stereo. The drag off a pilfered cigarette. All those things helped ward off that annihilating quiet.

MY FRIENDS

I had two friends at the beginning of sixth grade: my best friend Heather, who now lived in Fort Myers and came to stay for extended periods of time whenever we could talk one of our mothers into making the nearly two-hour round trip; and Erica, a girl I met at the bus stop, who lived on the next street over, who I sometimes hung out with but not often, as her mother didn't care for me, having found out my sister did drugs and my mother was crazy, which all reflected, somehow, on me.

FIRST KISS

When I was in the sixth grade, I got my first kiss. The boy who gave it to me went to school with my sister. I didn't like him, but when he showed up in our driveway one day after school, I didn't know how to tell him to leave. Somehow we ended up alone in my sister's bedroom. The boy didn't say a word as he sat next to me on the bed. I didn't say a word, either. I simply sat as still as possible, wishing that the oppressive quiet of the house would swallow me up. His tongue tasted like a raw hot dog. By the time he was done with me, my whole face was wet. This happened again and again for weeks, until one of my sister's other friends found out and threatened to kick his ass if he didn't leave me alone.

DEPRESSION

In my room, I listened to Pink Floyd's "The Wall." I was obsessed with "Mother." I hovered over the turntable, and as soon as Roger Waters sang the last mournful line, I lifted the arm and set it back to the song's start, the needle crackling as it found its groove. My mother, I was convinced, was going to make all my nightmares come true. To ward off the looming fear and sadness, I wrote poetry that I thought terribly poignant but deep down knew was just terrible. This made me feel worse. I was ugly and awkward and always on the verge of tears. You'd think someone would notice, but I got straight As and was never in trouble, so apparently there was nothing to worry about.

LAURA

Like everything else of my sister's, her best friend Laura would eventually become mine. She was 16 and lived two streets over. She wore Gloria Vanderbilt perfume. The bottle came in a purple box and had a swan etched into the glass. If I were to say Laura smelled like a purple swan, it wouldn't make much sense to anyone, but she did and it was lovely. I showed my most poignant poem, "The world is cold and lonely, and I'm the person only …" to Laura after she asked me one day what I did in my room alone all the time. Laura told my sister she thought I was depressed. My sister already knew but didn't know what to do about it.

NEW FRIENDS

Laura took me under her proverbial wing. I donned a denim

jacket just like hers and tucked my pack of Marlboro Lights that she bought for me into the breast pocket. The new friends Laura introduced me to seemed to come in pairs. Chris and George. Doug and Kevin. And (the lone loner), Doug's older brother Frank. Also, two other boys, John and his weird friend who would tell me on more than one occasion how he'd like to drink the blood of Ozzy Osbourne.

CHRIS AND GEORGE

Chris was a 16-year-old boy with light brown hair that fell in waves around his gorgeous smiling face. His smile was warm and dimpled and made me absolutely sick. Though still in high school, he worked as a house painter with George, a 20-something-year-old who could have been the living incarnation of Shaggy from Scooby Doo. He was tall and thin, perpetually stoned and incomprehensible.

DOUG AND KEVIN

Doug and Kevin had been friends since grade school. Their parents were also friends and ran in the same circles. They went to Cape High with Laura and Chris. Doug was beautiful in a dark way, with a bright, seldom-seen smile and lush hair. He was broody and rarely hung out in my sister's bedroom with us, though he was always on the periphery of our group. Kevin had thick curly hair and dimples like Chris, which showed often because he was so often smiling. Sometimes the two of us would sit in my mother's VW Bug late at night talking about poetry and philosophy and what meaning this life might have for us, if any.

RIVERHEAD CANALS

The streets we lived on—me, Erica, Doug, Frank, Kevin and Laura—were surrounded on three sides by the north, west and south Riverhead Canals. We were not boxed in, but were we nestled? The canals (which I never knew had names) led to other canals, and some of those canals led to the river, which led to the Gulf. The canals smelled of fish and salt and muck. Sometimes we'd see manatees making their peaceful way through the murky water with boat-propeller scars on their broad, sloping backs.

SOMEWHERE ELSE

Every one of us was from somewhere else. My sister and I and Erica were from Ohio. Doug and Frank were from New York. Kevin and Laura too. Chris was from Indiana. Heather was from Pennsylvania. Even John and his weird friend (and probably George) were from some state up north. There we all were, products of people who had left other lives behind, trying to make our own way.

AGAINST ALL ODDS

Heather and I wandered the neighborhood in the middle of the night holding a transistor radio between us, surfing the channels to find whatever station was playing "Against All Odds." When we found it, we'd sing as loud as we could, and my heart nearly broke every time within the first two lines. On that quiet street, nestled between the Riverhead Canals, with our voices marking our place in that vast, surprising world, I believed, if only for a moment, that no one would ever walk away again. No one would ever leave without a trace.

LOVE
Laura went out with Doug then fell in love with Frank. Frank liked Laura but didn't love her, so Laura eventually forgot about Frank and fell in love with Chris. George secretly loved Laura. I didn't know when Doug started to love me.

MORE LOVE
I loved Laura. And I loved Chris. I didn't know who I loved more. The little girl I had been was drawn to Laura, my surrogate mother. The grown-up girl I was becoming longed for Chris, though it hurt to look at him. "If you were just a little older, Amos," he would tell me, but I knew he was just being nice. At night, in my bed, I imagined him looking at me the way he looked at Laura. His fingers tucking a stray hair back in place behind my ear. Then his soft lips on mine, the kiss warm and gentle. Thinking of it made me feel afraid, but not in a bad way. It was only scary because it was new and because I wanted it so much.

JON K.
He was a nice man my mother met at The Clock, the first of many coffee shops she would come to haunt. Like all men, he adored my mother. He adored my sister and me too, even though my sister was sometimes rotten and stole his car. ("I always brought it back," she reminded me.) My mother let Jon move in,

no doubt, because he was down on his luck and my mother had a soft spot for such people. She herself was such a person, having had only, according to the marriage settlement agreement, $278 to her name ($195 of it in savings accounts for my sister and me), and over $6,000 in debt, not including rent and utilities. Jon likely helped her as much as she helped him. He kept the kitchen stocked with food other than Doritos and Pudding Pops. He referred to himself as a "Polack" and told us he used to be a race car driver, forced to retire after a career-ending crash. To prove this, he showed us his stump of a hand. Sometimes he'd wear his fake hand and wait for one of us to notice, laughing when we did.

SCHOOL CLOTHES

Jon took my sister and me school clothes shopping the summer before seventh grade. It was one of the few times anyone bought us clothes from a store. Most times, our clothes came out of a garbage bag someone had dropped off at the house. Jon took us to Burdines, no less, a high-end store where the girls in my grade who snickered in front of my face went shopping. The year we were in Ohio, my stepmother had taken us to a store where most of the tags were stamped "irregular." The new clothes Jon bought me hung in my closet, looking lonely and out of place. Spotless polo shirts in various colors, Jordache jeans with gleaming seams, a sleeveless cerulean blue sweater. The clothes smelled funny to me, and when I wore them to school, I felt like an imposter. The girls snickered all the more. "Nice try."

PURPLE BEAN BAG CHAIR

In the family room for a time there was a purple beanbag chair I bought at a garage sale for a dollar. I laid in it in the evenings, doing my homework, which I did diligently and enjoyably. I still loved school, despite the snickering girls. After my work was done, I settled back in the beanbag and watched wrestling with Jon. Andre the Giant, Dusty Rhodes, Rowdy Roddy Piper, The Iron Sheik. When Jimmy Snuka climbed the ropes for his Superfly Splash, Jon jumped off the couch, his stump waving excitedly in the air. From the floor, I waved my own hand, covered in Doritos dust.

CATS

We had three cats: a gray kitten we named Opie, a black and white one we named Ernie, and my sister's white cat, Spooky. Except for Spooky, who had been my sister's best friend since she was 10, the cats weren't special. We played with them until we got bored or distracted or sad and they were left to their own devices. It must have been Jon who cleaned their litter box and fed them, though who knows who took over once he moved out.

A TRIP

Laura and I were with some of our other friends, partying in my sister's bedroom. Everyone was smoking weed except me because Laura wouldn't let me. We were all drinking wine that someone had stolen from the corner store. Lancer's or Boone's Farm. Maybe Mad Dog. The stereo was blasting classic rock and when The Doors came on, Laura and I shrieked. At some point, my mother appeared in the doorway and peered in through the thick cloud of incense, cigarette and weed smoke. She wore an orange velour robe with flowing sleeves. She looked like a large, confused bird. We all stared at her. This was a rare sighting; she so rarely ventured back to this part of the house. "What are you kids doing?" she asked. Whatever we answered must have been enough, for my mother turned and swooped away. "Your mom's a trip," one of my friends said, and I agreed, then promptly forgot about her. I had other things to focus on, like making Laura laugh.

LAURA'S LAUGH

Laura's laugh was the sound of the world settling into place, and of me settling into it.

UNOFFICIAL FOSTERING

I stayed at Laura's house more and more. By seventh grade, I would eat dinner and do my homework there. We would watch the nightly lineup of TV dramas and Johnny Carson and then go to bed in Laura's room, her waterbed tossing us around, as she said, "I love you, Amos," before closing her eyes to sleep.

PERIOD

In her bathroom, Laura taught me to insert a tampon. I had just gotten my first period. I went through nearly half a box before I got the hang of it. Laura laughed her bubbly, bouncy laugh. "My little Amos is all grown up now." That night, Laura and

Chris and George took me to a pop-up carnival on Del Prado Boulevard to celebrate my womanhood.

AND THE LITTLE ONE SAID

Chris and Laura and I were in my bed. They were likely drunk, or stoned, or both. Laura was in the middle. I wished it were a different arrangement. I thought of a childhood song: "There were 10 in the bed and the little one said, 'roll over, roll over.'" Laura and Chris rolled over into each other, away from me, their lips making soft smacking sounds. The bed shook gently with their slow undulations. "There was one in the bed and the little one said, 'I'm lonely, I'm lonely.'"

MOVING OUT

We moved out of the house on Southeast 30th Street. My mother was upset because we would not get the security deposit back. The screen was busted out of my sister's bedroom window. There were holes in many of the cheap, hollow doors. There were cigarette burns in the carpet in the family room. We were leaving that house, but not without a trace.

Mom, After

When I compared the photograph of my mother post-breakdown to the picture of my mother in the trailer pre-breakdown, I was surprised that the smile was still the same. My mother shouldn't have still looked this happy, this unworn, unweathered.

The picture was stamped December 1983 on the back. So much had happened in that previous year. A first psychotic break, multiple hospitalizations, shock treatments, separation, upheaval, a second marriage. How did she still look so chirpy? It was not at all how I remembered her from Southeast 30th Street, the house where the second picture was taken. Maybe she and her second husband were still getting along; they wouldn't divorce until March the following year. Maybe he was not on the couch yet. Maybe they were still sharing a bedroom. Or maybe it was just that she'd already had her annual Kahlúa and cream; it was Christmastime.

I had more memories of my mother from Southeast 30th Street than I did from the trailer. But they all involved a more ghostly figure, not the smiling woman in the rocker. Was ghostly too melodramatic a word? Perhaps it was quiet; perhaps it was distant; perhaps it was aloof. She was there physically, but she always seemed to be somewhere else. Preoccupied.

But what memories did I have of us? Who did we become after her breakdown?

I recalled standing in the foyer of a large department store in Cape Coral. It might have been Zayre's. Maybe Kmart. We must have been waiting on my sister, for we sat there, just the two of us, on benches across from each other. She pulled a cigarette out of her pack, and I asked if I could have one. "I smoke now," I told her. I was maybe all of 13. Without batting an eyelash, she tapped one out for me and we lit up. Perhaps this was the moment when our relationship shifted. When we became something other than mother and daughter.

I recalled my mother playing Trivial Pursuit with Heather and me. She'd do that sometimes, when she wasn't tired from working all day, when she wasn't going out on a date, when she wasn't in the middle of a freak-out. I don't know why we played with her; she always won, even when Heather and I tried to stump her with made-up questions. "What makes Crystal Gayle's brown eyes blue?" Heather and I would stifle our giggles as my mother thought long and hard, rubbing the mole on her face as the cigarette smoldered in her other hand. After an excruciating amount of time, during which I wondered if she was perhaps on the verge of a freak-out, she looked our way and said simply, "It." Technically, she was right. Unaware of the joke, she reached for the dice and rolled again.

I recalled Heather and me fighting the flu together in my sister's bedroom. My sister didn't live there then; she was staying with her future first husband. Heather and I were in my sister's bedroom because it was closest to the bathroom. We'd been sick for what seemed like days, writhing on the floor convinced that we would die, dragging ourselves periodically to the bathroom to poop and puke simultaneously. One of us in the toilet and the trash can; the other in the bathtub and on a towel. It was a horror show (one Heather would confirm in a text some 25 years later when we reconnected: "How could one ever forget that?"). My mother came back to the room at least once, to offer lukewarm tea with chunks of non-dairy creamer floating on the top. She must have brought a bottle of Pepto-Bismol because I recalled how good and cold the thick pink liquid felt going down my dry, parched throat; my mother always kept the Pepto in the fridge. For a few seconds, I thought I might be OK. Sickness, at last, averted. Then the fists were back in my belly, squeezing and twisting my guts. Before I knew it, Heather and I were in the bathroom again exploding from both ends. I missed the towel completely when I threw up, leaving a bright pink puddle on the tan bathroom carpet.

I recalled tucking my mother into bed one night. Though I stayed at Laura's through the school week, I came back in the mornings to shower and change clothes, and sometimes in the evenings to tuck my mother in. How often was sometimes? Once? Never? It was surely somewhere short of always. On at least this one night that I recalled, my mother nestled into bed, letting me tuck the sheets and comforter around her as I cooed and made a tender fuss. Smoothing her hair back gently, I let my fingers sink into her thick, wooly hair; it felt like putting my hand in the flour canister. This person who so often seemed a ghost felt real, or at least familiar, as I bent down to plant a kiss.

The images that these memories painted showed a closeness of sorts, dysfunctional as it was. But I still couldn't reconcile the person in my mind with the smiling figure in the photograph. In it, she was sitting outside my bedroom door, in the rocker where she often sat at night holding a bag of Doritos, her eyelids heavy and her face slack from psychotropic sedation. She'd clutch a chip in her shaky hand and try to get it into her mouth, which would hang open, stuporous. My sister and I would laugh as a pile of chips grew in her lap.

"Did we really laugh?" I asked my sister. "That's so mean."

"We always laughed."

I saw myself in her face more than I saw her. I had her eyes, her smile. I did not, thank God, have her hair. If I covered the right half of her face with my hand, it was me I was looking at. So, why did I feel so distant from her? We shared a birthday. We looked so similar. I came from her. I was once a part of her.

And how was it that she didn't she look as sad or lonely or gone as I remembered her? What was wrong with my brain? My memory?

But then, I saw it. It jumped out at me like a ghost. The shadow. How many times had I seen that photo and never noticed the blackness hovering behind her, to her left, just outside my bedroom door? I felt a surge of emotions and was reminded of a line from a story I wrote years ago: "... gripped by a fear that makes me sad." The shadow was the mother I knew; I didn't remember the woman in the rocker.

Six:

1985 to 1989, Florida

Embrace

I t was 1987, and I was 15 years old. I had been Doug's girlfriend for a year. One particular night, I was with him and some of his rough and wild friends while they partied in a field next to a canal in Cape Coral. Orange 107 FM was blaring classic rock from one of the car stereos. Some people were jumping into the canal for a midnight swim. During the day, if the sun was just so, you could see crabs in the water scurrying across jagged chunks of submerged concrete. At night, you couldn't see anything at all. I wanted to be nowhere near that water, day or night.

I was sitting on the hood of someone's car, away from the fray. I was probably looking at the stars. Maybe composing a poem in my head. I was a dreamy girl.

While I was sitting, staring or composing, the wildest, roughest man, Tovat, a 20-something curly-blond-haired devil, came up from behind and grabbed me around the waist and off the hood, pulling me toward the water, laughing, threatening to throw me in. In an instant, I thought about those crabs. I thought about darkness and coldness and jagged chunks of concrete. I screamed. I kicked and flailed. I thrashed wildly in Tovat's strong, gorgeous arms until suddenly—he stopped. His grip around my waist closed in, but softly, like an embrace. I whimpered, hoarse. Tears blurred my vision. My breath came in short gasps. He pulled me tighter and whispered in my ear. "Shh. It's OK." I was startled by how quickly I felt safe again.

At Sea

S ometime in the spring of 1985, my mother, my sister and I
moved out of the house on Southeast 30th Street and into
a duplex on Skyline Boulevard at the corner of Southwest 22nd
Terrace, near the Bolero and Challenger canals.

A photograph was taken the year before that move, in 1984.
It would have been my father or Nancy who snapped the shot
from the balcony of the Lani Kai during one of their summer

trips to stay with us at Fort Myers Beach. I remembered it as a good visit; no one fought too much. In the mornings my father gave me money and sent me across the street to buy Pinwheels and milk from the 7-Eleven. I spent the days in the Gulf, floating on a raft or collecting sand dollars with my feet, my toes turning yellow orange from the iodine. One day, my sister and I chased after Nancy's hat, which had blown off her head, and we found it way down the beach. When we picked it up, a baby octopus the size of a pill bottle scurried back into the water. In the evenings, my sister and I played Ms. Pac-Man on the tabletop machine in the hotel lobby. She was a master at it (she had memorized the winning routes for each level), and she beat me every time.

The picture captured me floating alone on my raft in the Gulf of Mexico, one hand trailing lightly in the water. Whoever snapped the shot did so at just the right time for the sunlight to flare on my left, and whoever developed it did so in just such a way for light to band on my right, leaving the impression that I was nestled in this particular time and space, though there was water all around me.

On the back, Nancy wrote "Amy at Sea" in one corner and "August '84" in the other. What was I thinking in that captured moment? What was I feeling? I doubted I was sad—then—about being all alone, at sea. This was the summer of 1984, after all, and I knew Laura and all our friends waited for me at home. I had my own good life with people I loved who loved me. The future felt promising, with so many adventures ahead of me. I did not know that in less than a year I would be—would feel, at least—so adrift.

For over 30 years I referred to our place on Skyline as "North Cape Coral," an isolated part of the city 800 miles away from Southeast 30th Street. But it's not North Cape Coral. The adjacent Southwest 22nd Terrace told me as much. In fact, according to the online map I consulted, the distance between our old house and our new duplex was only six miles; under five with the new Veterans Memorial Parkway. In my memory's defense, Southwest Cape Coral wasn't much more populated in the mid-1980s than North Cape Coral, west or east. The houses were scattered across the flat, scrubby terrain. The high school was close, sure, but seemed far thanks to the canals that blocked the most direct routes. There was a Circle K a few streets away, but there were no fast food restaurants, no strip malls, no banks, no churches. No nothing, it seemed to me.

The duplex was a nondescript one-story without a garage. Our unit was on the left, nearest the side street. It had two bedrooms, two bathrooms, a living room, an eat-in kitchen, a screened back porch. In my mind, the surrounding landscape was bare and barren, vacant and forsaken, bleak, oppressive, dreary, austere. There weren't enough adjectives to convey how desolate that place seemed to me. According to pictures of the duplex and its surroundings, however, there were many green things, palms and palmettos and various pines. In the distance to the west, there was even a stretch of woods. Still, to me, then, it seemed a wasteland.

I could not remember exactly when we moved. I'd been trying to get the timeline down for years, literally, since my gathering began, but without distinct memories and with Florida's distinctless seasons, it was hard to know. But I needed to know.

We were definitely on Southeast 30th Street at the beginning of seventh grade, the fall of 1984. Jon K. took us school clothes shopping then. That was a fact. While I didn't remember the shopping trip, I remembered the clothes. I wore the sleeveless cerulean blue sweater for picture day that year. I dug my Gulf Middle School yearbooks out to verify this. Yes, there I was. Seventh grade. Cerulean blue sweater.

Another clue: my yearbook from seventh grade, which I would've gotten in the spring of '85, had the Skyline address written in it, along with our new phone number.

Then there was this: a note I wrote to my friends in June of '85, which I could only assume by the contents was written after we moved. I never gave it to anyone but kept it for myself. I eventually typed it up and included it in my "Collected Works" that my father helped me put together when I was a senior in high school. The note was one more chance object that had managed to survive many years.

Though it read like a suicide note, it wasn't.

Friday Night 6/?/85

I'm just sitting here thinking about all the good times that
we've had. We were all so close; we were like one big family. You
guys were my family. From you I learned things that no one else
could teach me. We shared good times, as well as bad times. We
laughed together, we cried together, we talked together. I miss
you all so bad. I always thought that you'd be here with me. But
I guess the young expect too much out of life, like I did. I guess
I was too naive and way too blind. But I think I chose to be blind,
because veiwing life as it is is much too painful. I used to feel
like I had a reason to be here. I thought I was put here to put a
little happiness in your lives; to put back some of the innocence
that we all seem to lose along the way. But now I have no reason
to be here, because I can't even make myself happy. And I really
don't feel all that innocent anymore. I just feel like I'm drifting
from place to place, not quite sure where I'm going or where I'm
from. Life has no apparent reason anymore. Before, I wanted to make
all of you happy all of the time, because I always was. It seems
corny, but... I just don't know. I guess I'm just lonely, because
I was special then. Everyone seemed to want me around and to care
about me. I've never felt like that before. I felt like everyone's
child and friend and whatever... Now I'm just here, and sometimes
I feel like I'm in the way. I never felt in the way back then. I
always felt secure and protected, like no one could harm me. Now
I just feel scared. I guess I'll go now. See ya...

                                                        Amos

I was at Erica's house when I originally wrote it. While
she and her other friend practiced dance moves to the newest
Madonna song, I scrawled the words on a piece of loose-leaf
torn from Erica's notebook. Or maybe on the back of a label
peeled carefully off the wine cooler I was drinking. It was hard
to say if I was drunk when I wrote it. While I did drink in middle
school, I didn't drink often, and I didn't drink a lot. Usually, I
drank just enough to feel that warm, glowy sadness. A feeling
akin to putting my hand in the flour canister; there was a softness
to it, even a sense of safety. Like being under glass, behind more

glass. In that bleary place of not-quite-drunk, there was a certain clarity sobriety could not offer. Like being able to see a star that's usually only visible obliquely, peripherally.

What intrigued me—comforted me, really—was the way this small piece of writing confirmed the themes that had emerged in my gathering up to that point. My lifelong search for belonging, safety, comfort. I hadn't just made all that up looking back over the course of a lifetime. I wasn't just reading into old photographs what I wanted. This was proof of how I felt in the moment as that 13-year-old girl, separated again from those she considered family.

And though I hoped it would also complete the triangulation and nail down the exact date or at least month of our move, I arrived back where I had started, sometime in the spring of 1985.

Why was it so important for me to know exactly when we moved? What difference would it make? Why had I wasted countless hours poring over my middle school yearbooks for time clues, doing mostly fruitless Internet searches for a divorce decree and possible eviction proceedings, asking my sister for clarification though her memory had always been worse than mine when it came to this era? Why did I pay $30 to do a background check on my dead mother, hoping to find a reliable address history? It was the most obsessed I had been since my gathering began. Why?

Perhaps it was my way of calming the anxiety that resurfaced when I thought about yet another big event of which I had such little memory. Perhaps I wanted an exact date so I could get closer to a sense of being, if not on solid ground, then at least temporarily anchored.

Why we moved out of the big, sparsely furnished house on Southeast 30th Street was as clear then as it was years later: money. How many times had I heard my mother crying on the phone to bill collectors? Or to my father, telling him, "I just can't do this anymore, Thom." Sometimes she would yell, telling him he had to come get us. Sometimes she'd plead for more child support.

I remembered practically nothing about the packing or the actual moving. Only one thing remained in my memory of that move: Laura and I walking through the house one last time, checking to make sure we had gotten everything. When we got to my mother's room, I opened the door to her walk-in closet. One of the cats (Ernie, I believe) jumped out of the dark at me, his eyes wild and mouth foaming, a strong ammonia smell of cat urine wafting over me. I tried to hold him, to comfort him, but he wriggled free, scratching my arms and face as he did. How long had he been in that dark place all alone? Where had he run off to? I didn't know. What I did know was this sad fact: we left him behind.

My sister and I were supposed to share the second bedroom on Skyline, but her future first husband usually stayed the night, so I slept on one of the small sectionals his father gave us when we moved. Whenever my mother kicked my sister out or she stormed out, I'd get the room to myself. Who knows how many times that happened. My sister's comings and goings. It was likely that by the beginning of my ninth-grade year, my sister was gone for good—she bounced her way back and forth from Laura's house to her future first husband's house until her senior year, when she got pregnant, quit school, and got her own place.

During those early days on Skyline, my sister and I did the grocery shopping, taking the $50 or $60 my mother gave us each week ($20 of it allocated for her carton of cigarettes; kids could buy them for their parents back then) and heading into town in my mother's enormous brown Ford LTD. We always shopped in the middle of the night, after my mother took her pills and went to bed. Sometimes, my sister would let me drive and I'd sit up as tall as I could, willing myself to look several years older anytime we came close to passing a cop.

This early Skyline era could have been referred to as the pre-Tom Mayle era. Before the man who would become my second stepfather moved into our lives, my mother was much as she had been on Southeast 30th Street: a smoking, working and apparently smiling ghost. She hung out with her various man friends at The Clock, then O'Hare's, and when she wasn't at one of these coffee shops, she was at our kitchen table drinking coffee with various man friends. I called them coffee shops because that's what my mother did there; she drank coffee. But they were actually small diners—greasy spoons, as my mother would describe them—with Formica on the tabletops and American fare on the menu.

The man friends were always nice to us. I couldn't remember any of them being creeps, not even the two ex-cons, Skip and Ron. But none of them stuck around once my mother had one of her freak-outs. As soon as the pacing and the staring started—and the smoking, always the smoking—the man friends would split and my mother would retreat into her room, which was even darker in the duplex than in the big house we had come from. Meanwhile, our world of underage drinking, blaring stereos, and friends coming and going at all hours, went on.

When my mother did venture out of her room to pace and smoke, my sister and I took turns skipping school and following her around the house with an ashtray so she wouldn't burn the place down. Then one of us would think to call our Uncle Myke, who'd come by to knock her out with a beer.

Such was life pre-Tom Mayle.

There was fighting then, too. Between my sister and her future first husband; between my mother and my sister; between me and my sister. Once, my sister and her future first husband were fighting and he hit her. My mother stepped between them to defend her daughter and threatened to call the police. My sister—not surprisingly—turned against my mother to defend her future first husband. There was slapping and screaming and lots of name calling. I ended up calling Laura's mother, who came to fetch me, and she encouraged my sister to leave, too. Then she turned to my mother and berated her for being a terrible parent. My mother by this time was crying helplessly, so confused. As I remembered how worn and dejected she had looked, my heart ached. I had wanted to defend her, but I didn't know how then. I wasn't very good at it now. Part of me did blame my mother. If only she were normal, I thought, we all maybe could have a chance.

I often ended up at Laura's house, even after we moved, bumming rides from my mother or my sister, or on that one occasion, carted there by Laura's mother. It wasn't the same, though. Laura had, by this time, distanced herself from our old group and had new friends, girls in her grade who used designer hairspray instead of Aqua Net and bought their clothes new from the mall. These new friends were popular girls, not stoners, like our other friends. This new group of friends had no place for a flat-haired 13-year-old in a Doors T-shirt. Many nights, I'd watch Laura get ready to go to a party. As she brushed bright blue powder on her pale lids, she'd eye me pouting in the mirror. "I still love you, Amos," she would say. "I just need my own space."

Laura was still going out with Chris. He lived with her now, and when I was at her house—a new house, as her family had moved as well—it was Chris who got to sleep in her waterbed, while I crashed on the couch in the family room or the pull-out in the living room, depending on where any of the other drifters Laura's family took in happened to crash that night.

When I wasn't at Laura's, I could be found at my grandparents' condo, swimming in their pool or walking the length of the canal looking for chameleons. I also started working that summer. One job was at my grandparents' condo community. My grandfather paid me $5 an hour to clean the clubhouse once a week. It only took 30 minutes to clean; it was never dirty. But my grandfather paid me the full $5, nonetheless. I also had babysitting gigs and sometimes even went to work with my mother at a print shop, where the owner would pay me $5 an hour to collate the papers shucking out of the big copiers. I loved that job the most. The opportunity to bring order to chaos.

Sometimes I'd go to The Clock and then later O'Hare's with my mother and sit and listen to her man friends chatter on while my mother sat quietly, drinking her coffee and smoking her cigarettes, occasionally nodding her head and smiling at something one of them said. Some of them called her Susie, some Sue. My mother joked she'd answer to anything but "late for dinner." While it wasn't always easy to be with her, it was easy to be with her and her man friends. I liked these times with my mother. I liked sitting at a table or at the counter with them, sipping my pop and reading a book. I felt safe and almost whole. My mother, in their presence, seemed real to me. And in their presence, I felt real to her. It seemed that in the company of these men, we could be as they saw us, as we once had been—a mother and a daughter.

Of all my friends from Southeast 30th Street, Doug and Kevin were the only ones to visit. Doug had a car, and I used to love hearing its engine gun as he revved it one last time before parking on the oily patch of dead grass to the side of the duplex. Sometimes we'd drive out to the real North Cape Coral and ride through the houseless neighborhoods, where the streets sprouted weeds so high, they scraped the undercarriage of Doug's Malibu. Where the faded street signs flashed white in the headlights. Where the power lines hummed softly in the night.

School was school. I still enjoyed the work, except for science. My friend Erica had also moved out to Skyline that year—though on the opposite end of the boulevard—and while we rode the same bus, we weren't in any classes together. I was on the college-bound track. They started that early at Gulf Middle School, pegging kids in the sixth grade, predicting which ones would likely make it academically beyond high school. I was one of those kids. But while I got good grades and tested well, I didn't belong to any groups or clubs or even the honor society. I wasn't a total outsider, though. The autographs from my Gulf Middle yearbooks showed that other kids knew who I was and even liked me. One girl seemed to really know me: "You remind me of the movie 'Angel.' Quiet and nice in school and smoking and drinking out of school!" At any rate, I never ate lunch alone. But I never felt like I fit in with kids my age. They wore bright, new clothes and listened to Top 40. They complained about the unfairness of curfews and too-low allowances. I, meanwhile, carried a pack of Marlboro Lights in my purse and often ate Eggo waffles for dinner.

I was apparently normal enough to go on the ubiquitous eighth grade trip to D.C. I had vague memories of riding on a plane with my classmates and staying at a fancy hotel. Of walking through Georgetown and touring the Smithsonian. Of someone playing Foreigner on a portable cassette player on the bus ride to Arlington. The trip was around Easter, which in 1986 was on Mar. 30.

I knew the trip was around Easter because by the time our plane landed in Fort Myers and we made it back to Gulf Middle in Cape Coral, it was close to midnight. My sister was supposed to pick up Erica and me. The late hour wasn't a problem for my sister; she was a closer at the McDonald's on Del Prado and a night owl anyway. Erica and I watched as the other kids sought and found their parents among the crowd of parents. Watched them receive awkward one-arm hugs and in some cases a cheek kiss and full embrace. One by one, we watched everyone else pile into cars. I'm sure we must've lied to the last of the parents before they drove away. "Oh, yes. My sister will be here anytime now."

My sister never came. "I totally just forgot," she told me whenever I brought it up. "I kinda feel bad about that."

Erica and I had no choice but to walk to my house. Though I liked to pretend the walk took hours, when I plugged in Gulf

Middle School's address and my old Skyline address, I found the walking distance was only three miles, estimated to take just a little over an hour, even with those damn canals.

Twenty years ago, I wrote a story about this long walk home, thereby creating a memory of that experience for myself and ruining any chance of retrieving any actual memories. Only one actual memory survived in my brain from that night: When we finally made it home, there was a large package from Ohio waiting to be opened. In it were two large stuffed bunnies for my sister and me (one pink, one yellow) that my father had sent to us for—you guessed it—Easter.

I had absolutely no memory of the actual walk. I knew it happened. But knowing was not the same as remembering, and the not remembering continued to give me that lost, queasy feeling of being at sea, adrift in my own life.

Choosing My Own Adventure

P icture this: April 1986. A girl, just turned 14 and home from her eighth grade prom, fell for a boy because he fell for her. She fell in love with being loved. The boy, Doug, 18 and drunk, waited for her in the driveway of the duplex where she lived—adrift—in the wasteland that was at that time Southwest Cape Coral, Florida.

The girl had known the boy for several years and she was not afraid. This was the same boy who once, when she was 12, let her drink his beer and cry safely in his car as she wailed on about her crazy mother. He was the only friend from the old neighborhood who bothered to drive out to visit her now that she lived in that neglected place. He was the boy whose heart she'd break in three years. He was the one she'd leave. Like her mother left her father a mere decade before.

This girl was lonelier than a 14-year-old should be. Craving attention, she was primed for mistaking it for love.

They sat together in the living room on the sectional that was often her bed. Her mother was asleep. Her sister was out. She and the boy, alone. The boy held his head in his hands, or maybe laid it on her lap. "I love you," he said. "You're too young," he said. "I can't help myself," he said. His scent—that simple mix of boy sweat and beer—made her heart feel both heavy and light. Her stomach, too. He was handsome in a dark way that seemed attainable to her. This boy loved her? Her. With her big nose and flat hair. He was so drunk she felt sorry for him. She couldn't remember ever feeling so tender toward another human being.

She was surprised by this turn of events, but not in the way you might think. Sure, she had noticed before how he looked at her, hoped there might be something to his driving all the way out to what he and all their friends called Bumfuck, Egypt just to hang out with her. And there was that other night, not long before this one, when her mother's boyfriend bought her and her friends a keg, and her sister and sister's future first husband showed up fighting, and her sister put her fist through the glass, and the police were called. The boy had shown up then, just as the girl was starting to cry, to lose her breath.

The woman I became could still see Doug's face, framed by the front door's broken glass. How our eyes met from across the apartment. Corny, I know, but that's how it happened—at least how I remembered it happening. His eyes asked, "Are you OK?" And mine answered in an instant, "I am now."

So, on that night when I was 14 and home from my eighth grade prom—having gone dateless with Erica and her boyfriend and his friends—it was as though I knew Doug would be there waiting for me, telling me he loved me. I remembered how surprised I had felt that I had known.

I had known, also, that what I did in that moment would change the course of my life. Should I have sat and listened, or sent him away? I had a feeling somewhere between abandon and inevitability. It was different from the mixed feelings of obligation and helplessness I had had a few years before when that other older boy would show up after school at Southeast 30th Street and French-kiss me in my sister's bedroom. Then, I felt that being available to that gross, inappropriate boy was my duty, something I had no say in. With Doug, I had a feeling of something akin to fate. Yes, I had a choice to make, but I felt I already knew what that choice would be. And it was a big choice. The biggest, I thought, of my short life, since unlike the "Choose Your Own Adventure" books, I wouldn't be able to change my mind, go back. I would have to own my choice forever.

We all have to own our decisions, even when they seem so out of our control. There's always that moment. That one moment. What would my life have been if I had told Doug to go home and had simply gone inside, locked the door, and gone to bed? Would I have ended up with Doug anyway? Would I have ended up leaving him anyway? Because that's what I came to believe was the fated outcome of the choice I made that night: I had received him so I could leave him, thereby replaying the psychodrama of my mother leaving my father.

Despite my past infatuations with other boys—Matt Martell, Jason N., Laura's Chris—Doug truly was my first love. After that night of my eighth grade prom, he'd drive out to see me every night. I'd sit in the living room sick and giddy with anticipation, listening for the sound of his Malibu, waiting for him to open the front door, beer in hand, and flash me that smile he seemed to reserve just for me. He always wore corduroy pants, even in the height of summer, and was partial to button-down shirts, unbuttoned and untucked. He tended to brood when sober, but after a few beers (Doug almost always had a few beers in him), his manner was laid-back, his smile easy. He was slim and tan and handsome. Every time he showed up, I couldn't believe it was for me. Was this how my mother felt with my father back when they were still just two kids themselves? "I'm proud, yes proud, to be seen with you," she had written to him all those years ago.

During Doug's broody moods, when his smile would fade, and he'd seem grouchy and withdrawn, I'd tell myself this was the price for not being alone. And the sex I knew he was expecting, that too, I figured was a price.

Unlike my parents' fateful piece of pie, there was nothing impulsive about my first time. I knew even at 14 I had to protect myself, at least from pregnancy, which I equated then as the absolute ruination of lives. So I had my sister drive me to the free clinic on Anderson Avenue in Fort Myers, where the hookers and the junkies and other stray kids went, so I could get on birth control pills.

I waited a full cycle before I felt safe enough. In the meantime, Doug talked me into oral sex. Could he have said something as banal as "it's OK, just put your mouth on it" all the while wagging it around between two fingers? At any rate, I did, many times. Once, the morning before my first day of summer school after eighth grade (I had opted to go to get a jump on high school—I liked to be ahead of things), my mother had spent the night at a boyfriend's house, and my sister and her future first husband were in the other bedroom, so Doug and I slept in my mother's bed. After I was done putting my mouth on it, Doug rolled over to go back to sleep while I got ready for school. As I was doing my makeup, my mother came into the bathroom, looking confused. "Does that boy have pants on?" I had no idea what to say.

I was in my own bed when I finally lost my virginity. It was a little later into that summer after eighth grade. Before ninth grade sounds better. What might be the exact date would be best: Jun. 12, 1986.

The date came by way of a photograph of Doug and me on which Sept. 12, 1986, our three-month anniversary, was noted on the back.

What better event to mark an anniversary? According to Google, it was a Thursday. While we did it, Pink Floyd's "Comfortably Numb" played on the radio.

It hurt at first, but I got used to it. There was a feeling of embarrassment on my part, maybe fear. "There's no going back now," I could imagine myself thinking. Mostly there was a feeling of uncertainty. I could feel it in the two-line poem I wrote nearly a month later commemorating the event: "Did I lose or did I gain? Was there love within the pain?"

What would I have said to this young, lonely girl aching for attention? Would I have told her to wait? To not give herself away so easily? I didn't think I could have. The whole thing with Doug had that air of inevitability to me. But did it, really? Or was I just an awkward, naive girl who fell for the first boy to look at her twice? He loved me. How many girls had fallen for that trick?

He did love me, though. There was not one iota of doubt about that. He loved me. He would have married me if I had let him, and lived happily ever after, too.

I was sure I didn't ponder any of this on that night in June 1986. I was sure I just clenched my jaw and tried to swivel my hips so he wouldn't tell our friends I was a dead fuck. I didn't think he would have said that to anybody even if I had lain stock-still; Doug wasn't like that. But at the time, I couldn't be sure.

I remembered thinking of my father. The thought was as clear then as Roger Waters' voice coming from my radio. I could hear the three hellos followed by my "Bye Dad." I imagined I felt sad. I had always felt sad when I thought about saying goodbye to my father. His little girl was gone now for good.

It was not like I was close to my father at the time. He still lived in Ohio with Nancy. We still saw them at least once a year, but our visits had become tense. My sister and I were both in a phase where we'd only wear black T-shirts with rock band logos. My father thought we looked like hoodlums, though he hadn't used that word. My sister, whenever she was asked if she liked something, had the new and purposefully annoying habit of replying, "It's giving me an orgasm."

During one visit around this time, we were in what had been a happy place for us: my father's stained glass workshop. He was helping us pick out colors to frame a mirror we were going to make for Laura. He asked if she had her own room or shared it with a sister. My sister and I looked at each other for a moment, then giggled. "She shares it with her boyfriend, Chris." From our perspective, it was the most normal thing in the world for a 16-year-old girl to have her boyfriend living with her. My sister had been living with her boyfriend for some time, though my father didn't know that, and I had Doug staying with me when I had the room to myself. We knew better though, than to ever let on how things were in Florida with our mother. Even though normal for us, we knew in my father's world, this kind of behavior would be shocking.

It had indeed shocked my father. "That's disgusting," he said, and asked what kind of lives we were living down there, and with what kind of people. The mirror for Laura never got made.

Was I as mad about this moment as I became later? I didn't remember. But by my late teens and early 20s, I was fighting often with my father in my head about such things he had said to us, the insinuating remarks that our lives as children were of our own choosing. "You're our father!" I'd yell in my mind. "Why didn't you do something about how we were living?"

In fairness, what would we have let him do? Whenever he came for his annual visits, we were careful to hide the truth. We'd clear my sister's drug paraphernalia, tell our friends who were used to coming at all hours to stay away, empty our mother's overflowing ashtrays, give the house a half-assed cleaning, and act as normal as we could so as not to raise suspicion that we were basically living unattended.

And, in more fairness, he did once ask me to come live with him. He had found out somehow that I had been staying at Laura's house most of the time, a house not only where girls were allowed to move their boyfriends in, but also where girls were plied with alcohol and cigarettes. (One year when I was 12, Laura's family gave me a carton of Marlboro Lights in my Christmas stocking.)

How my father and I came to be sitting in his rental car alone on a side street of Cape Coral, I had no idea. Where was Nancy? Where was my sister? He shook his head, exasperated.

"I don't understand why you want to live like this." I wasn't sure how much he knew about Laura's house. Did he know Laura's mother was in a three-way marriage with her husband and her best friend? Did he know Laura's stepfather was an abusive alcoholic? Did he know about all the drifters they took in and how many times I slept on the couch in Laura's living room while strange men slept on the floor?

Maybe he wasn't talking about Laura's house at all. Maybe he was shocked by the way we were living with our mother. Our cramped apartment. Our cheap clothes. Our even cheaper furniture. Maybe he was upset by the things we didn't think to hide.

In my memory of this conversation with my father, I was sitting in the driver's seat and he was in the passenger's. But that couldn't be right. I wasn't nearly old enough to drive. I felt so bad telling him no, feeling somehow that I was abandoning him all over again. All I could do was cry and say I was sorry. But I didn't want to leave Doug or my sister or Laura or even my mother. To my relief, he didn't insist.

Despite his disgust and his disappointment, my father continued to send us gifts on the major and minor holidays, as well as trinkets throughout the year from all his IBM business trips. I used to have a Hard Rock Cafe pin from every major city in the country. I still thought of him fondly, though to me he seemed a little snooty and a lot naive. I wouldn't really hate him until college, after his multiple confessions about Callie Smith and sleeping with all my mother's friends.

But I couldn't be too hard on my father anymore, not after I discovered a crucial parallel to our stories: There was another boy.

I was 15 years old, starting my sophomore year at Cape High. The class was second year Latin.

I was still dating Doug who was, by then, 19, well out of high school and living in Tampa attending technical college. Dating was the wrong word. In the parlance of the day, we were going out, and going out was a serious thing, like marriage.

I wore acid-dyed jeans, French-cuffed, with socks to match my shirt. Sometimes I tucked my jeans into Bon Jovi-style tassel boots. I wore black leather peace sign earrings and carried my pack of Marlboros (Reds, now) and a roll of SweeTARTS in a purse with a leopard-skin flap. I had rings on every finger, and every nail was bitten to the quick. I liked hair metal, but my favorite all-time band was still The Doors. At home, my bedroom walls were plastered with posters of Jim Morrison. I was a strange amalgamation of the '80s and the '60s. I fit nowhere.

Joseph, the boy I would soon be madly in love with, was also 15. He sat in the back of Latin class, always alone, drawing action figures while the rest of us conjugated verbs. When he wasn't drawing action figures, he was reading. He was tall, with sharp elbows and feminine hands. He never slouched. Sometimes he wore an ROTC uniform and looked especially dorky. He was everything Doug was not. I would stare at him out of the corner of my eye and feel a quickening in my chest I knew was trouble. I was married, essentially; I belonged to someone. I wasn't supposed to want anything else.

I kept my eye on Joseph day after day, until one day I gathered enough courage to take the seat two seats away from him, leaving a desk between, just in case. The space between us felt electric.

"What are you reading?" I may have asked him. Likely, he glanced at me slowly, one eyebrow raised in that way I would come to love. The expression of that arched brow a mix of "Why are you bothering me?" and "Oh! What's this now?"

It could have been a Stephen King novel. Maybe a John Irving. Which one of us introduced the other to "The Hotel New Hampshire," the book that would become our book? I'd never seen a boy with a book before. Not true. In middle school, Brian Honaker and I would swap trashy horror novels, paper clipping the dirty parts (the demonic seductions and satanic orgies). But Brian had never made me feel like I felt then with Joseph.

Our Latin teacher that year was a short, tidy Cuban man who often went off on tangents about the Bay of Pigs, and the torture methods the American CIA had adopted from the Spanish inquisitors. Sometimes, he'd draw us diagrams. The iron maiden. The rack. The head crusher. The wheel.

During this strange 50 minutes five days a week, Joseph and I got to know each other. We discovered we both loved classic rock and hated '80s pop. We both had older siblings we had idolized but never wanted to become. I told him my mother was crazy and that I had been essentially married to someone much too old for me for over a year. He raised that one eyebrow in a way I took as him being impressed—this pleased me more than I knew it should. He told me he thought I was something else entirely, one of those vapid girls who loved listening to Top 40 and going to pep rallies.

We became friends. Not only were we in Latin, but we also had English and history together. Soon, Joseph and another boy, Scott, were constantly getting me and another girl, Stephanie, into trouble for making us laugh during class. The four of us quickly developed inside jokes about "The Good Earth" and "The Scarlet Pimpernel." About the French and Russian revolutions. About Shakespearean tragedies and "Beowulf." We defaced our textbooks with what would today be considered clever memes. For the first time, I felt like I truly fit in with kids at school. Tenth grade became a magical, parallel universe I got to live in while my other life outside of school went on.

My outside-of-school life consisted primarily of work and Doug. My mother had gotten me a dishwashing job at O'Hare's. It was my first real job and I took great pride in it, making sure to keep the plate stacks stacked and the silverware coming. I changed my sink water frequently to keep it fresh and hot even though Judy O'Hare bitched about how much water I wasted. I knew it was the right thing to do. Jim O'Hare sometimes came back to the kitchen to tell me my mother was at the counter drinking coffee. I'd notice a look come across his face, of pity, maybe wonder. If only I could go back and ask him what he thought of her, of us.

On weekends, Doug would drive the two hours south to stay with me at my mother's or else I'd hitch a ride north with my uncle to stay with Doug. No one seemed to worry that I was only 15 and he was 19. I certainly didn't worry; I was on the pill, after all.

Doug shared an apartment with two other guys. One, Junior, was a scuzzy degenerate who thought it was funny to ejaculate into other people's shampoo bottles. The apartment was unfurnished save for a folding table and mismatched wooden chairs from one of their grandmothers' kitchens. On the walls were taped centerfold pictures from "Hustler," "Swank" and "Oui." The pictures didn't shock me. My mother kept copies of "Oui" in her nightstand drawer. At Laura's house, her stepfather, her mother and their girlfriend kept various magazines in the living room side tables, magazines filled with black and white photographs that both excited and horrified.

One night I visited while Doug was at work. He had installed a deadbolt on the inside of his bedroom door to protect his stuff, and on that night, I must've forgotten to set the lock. I woke up to find a very drunk Junior face down in my crotch telling me what he would like to do to me if only I would let him. "I would treat you so good," he slurred. "You're so beautiful."

I was afraid, but more disgusted. Junior was a pale boy with sour skin and bad teeth. Even more, I was shocked. Beautiful was not a word I would have used for myself. I squeaked out a pitiful "no," and to my amazed relief Junior left without incident. When I could move, I got up and set the bolt.

In the morning, as though recounting a dream, I told Doug. His anger was sudden and surprising to me. I tried to tell him nothing happened. There was nothing to worry about. But he went and punched Junior in the face anyway, knocking out two of his bad teeth.

Doug had other friends, rough and wild men who always treated me with respect. Or maybe it was Doug they respected. It probably helped that I wasn't jealous or bitchy or high maintenance. I didn't demand Doug buy me expensive things or take me out on dates. I was always content doing whatever he wanted to do. If he wanted to play his guitar for hours or jam with his friends, I'd be there with him. If he wanted to work on his Malibu or one of his friends' cars, I'd be there with him. If he wanted to take a long drive or watch a movie, I'd be there with him. I was always there with him, even when my mind wasn't.

I never mentioned my school friends—or school—to Doug. He knew I took it seriously and would even tell me how proud he was of me. "My baby's so smart!" Doug himself was a different kind of smart; he could fix anything that broke and knew what all the stuff in Radio Shack was for.

The only person I talked to about my school friends was Laura.

"Joseph, Joseph, Joseph," she teased me one day on the phone. "You're in love with him!"

"I am not!"

"Amy loves Joseph!"

I reminded her I couldn't love Joseph; I was going out with Doug.

"You love him."

I remembered the day I knew she was right. I was walking the halls between classes, hoping to get a glimpse of Joseph before going into geometry when I ran into Scott. "Your boy isn't here today," Scott said, as though reading my mind. At that moment my face burned and my heart sank and I knew: I wanted something else.

I started to spend lunch in the library with Joseph, Scott and Stephanie. None of us really fit into any of the cliques represented in the cafeteria. Scott was an affable, popular nerd with lots of friends in various nerdy clubs, but because he chose to hang with us, he was deemed a partial outcast. Joseph had chosen total self-exile, taking great pride in never fitting in anywhere beyond our small group. Stephanie was seemingly normal, a straight-A student and clarinet player (or was it the violin?), but because she was Chinese American and a vocal Anglophile (with her love of Robert Smith, her overuse of the British "up yours" gesture, and the Union Jacks on her book covers), she too was relegated beyond the outer edges of popular social circles. We called ourselves the mutants, and our emblem was a one-eyed smiley face. Our slogan: "Mutants of the world unite!"

One day, we went around and shared what we thought of each other. The consensus was that I was someone who could've been popular, given different circumstances. I was surprised by this. Once I returned to Florida from Ohio and entered the sixth grade, I had felt like an instant outcast. Not quite a loser, but certainly no winner.

If I had stayed in North Royalton with my father and Nancy, perhaps I could've become that popular girl my friends saw in me. Perhaps I would've become a cheerleader or at least someone willing to go to a pep rally.

Though I didn't talk to my school friends much about my outside life, they knew just enough about my different circumstances to see how fate had failed me. I didn't think they'd understand. They were all virgins with seemingly normal parents, though Joseph's mother was once busted—with my mother—for smoking in the girl's bathroom during an award ceremony at the school. None of them had ever smoked a cigarette or gotten drunk. I doubted any of them had even kissed anyone. Though they were my closest friends in school, I still felt like an outsider. An outcast among outcasts. More so though, I kept my worlds apart because I didn't want to sully the thin illusion I had of fitting in with them. I wanted to maintain the space where I could believe I was just a normal girl who acted silly and laughed with her friends.

I really wanted to be a "normal" girl. One day, as I sat with Scott and one of his other friends between classes, they spoke about an upcoming dance and who they might ask. The friend glanced at me and said to Scott, "You could always ask Amy." Even though Scott wasn't Joseph, my heart fluttered, instantly imagining a scenario where I might be asked by a boy my age to go to something as normal as a school dance. "Nah," Scott answered quickly, "she's basically married." They both looked at me then, not unkindly, as though they were the ones missing out.

But it was me who was missing out, and I knew it. What could I do?

I tried to break up with Doug. Or at least I thought about trying to break up with him. My sister had come to pick me up one night, to do her grocery shopping, as she had long moved out by then. What had my sister said exactly? That's not going to be easy? She knew how things were. She was with her future first husband. Laura was with Chris. I was with Doug. Once you were with someone, you were theirs—at least until they were ready to be with someone else. And Doug wasn't ready to be with someone else. Doug, as I've said, loved me. Only me.

Instead of breaking up with him, I wrote him a poem, on May 24, 1988, not quite a month into the year that was supposed to be my sweetest. The poem affirmed how I loved him like I did before, with one little exception—I loved him more. Like my mother with my father all those many years ago, I embroidered a lie into a harmless untruth.

No matter how pretty my embroidery, though, I had begun to feel as trapped as I imagined both my mother and father felt on their wedding day. I couldn't see my possible futures, so much as feel them. The future with Doug felt stifling. The future without

Doug, exciting. With Doug, I would forever remain Doug's girl. Without Doug, who knows what I might become.

Thinking of my parents made me think of their wedding portrait, and that made me think of a photograph of Doug and me.

Looking at the image, I couldn't recall the occasion for which we'd dressed that way. Probably someone's wedding. I couldn't help but think of it as a prelude to our own wedding, which everyone—at least Doug and his parents—was expecting in a few years' time. Doug looked dapper in his sharkskin suit, while I looked presentable at best in an awful blue dress that I doubted was ever mine. I didn't even want to think about my shoes. My hair looked short, but it wasn't. Likely I had it up in a banana clip, that awful jaw-like contraption first popular in the late '80s.

I was probably 16 in the picture. That made Doug 20. We were two kids playing grown-up. I guessed it was his mother who snapped the picture, urging us to smile for the camera so she would have proof that even though her baby boy's girl was neither Catholic nor Italian nor of age, things appeared good and happy and as they should be.

It was not that we were unhappy. I knew Doug wasn't. It was evident by his smile. He looked proud. And I looked happy too, despite how awkward I must've felt in my fancy getup. Was I able to look that happy because of the secret life I was living in high school with Joseph and my other friends? Was the picture taken around the time Joseph gave me a birthday card: "Happy Sweet (yeah, right) Sixteen?" He had signed the card "love," and oh how I remembered my heart, fluttering and agitated, trying to reconcile the feelings I knew were dangerous. It was evident in a poem I wrote around that time:

"How would I enjoy it so
Like lips that kiss the morning light
That speak of promises of love
Youthful dreams and painless flight ..."

How smitten I was at 16, with Joseph. In love this time not just with being loved; I was in love with feeling in love.

If I had ever been in love with Doug, it was safe to say by

the time the photo was taken I wasn't any longer. I had my eye on something else. And that something else, I'd come to realize, wasn't even really Joseph. It was something Joseph represented. Normalcy, promise. A new and different adventure where I could be more than someone's girl. Where maybe I could be my own girl. My own normal girl.

The picture of Doug and me, like so many pictures I'd gathered, seemed revelatory to me. Although I was holding onto Doug, I was positioned just outside the background hallway arch that framed him. I was not enclosed. I was not surrounded. I was holding on and looking happy—maybe because part of me knew that soon I would be letting go.

Tenth grade ended, but the magic continued with Joseph through the summer. It was a summer of Joseph riding 10 miles round-trip on his bike out to Skyline nearly every day in baking heat to hang out with me; of him drinking pop I let go flat just for him, as he liked it that way; of the two of us sitting on my bed holding staring contests for hours, asking each other cryptically, "Do you love?" and answering just as cryptically, "Don't you know the answer?" Of writing Joseph poem after poem after poem, wallowing in the tragic romance of it all.

But then, summer ended. I still had not broken up with Doug, who was living in Cape Coral again. I had in fact written him more poems, too. Joseph by this time had outgrown his dorkiness, and thanks to all that cycling, was hot enough to get a real girlfriend for a while, a kind-of pretty girl named Karen. I was a coward. I had let the love of my young life slip through my hands. I had no one to blame but myself.

Eleventh grade started and was wholly unmagical. Joseph and Scott and Stephanie were in history class with me but nothing else. There were no more inside jokes. No more lunches in the library. I started buying SweeTARTS by the boxful and carried a bigger purse. I wrote new poems lamenting friendship's end, which were published in the school's literary magazine. My anatomy teacher asked me to autograph her copy, and I hated her for it. "You're going to be famous one day!" I thought she was mocking me; I was sure I wasn't ever going to be anything.

I got a new dishwashing job, at Annie's Restaurant, my mother's and Tom's—as this was now the Tom Mayle-era—new coffee shop. Annie's was a nice family restaurant, not a greasy spoon. The co-owner, who was Annie's ex-husband, used to joke that at O'Hare's they made their hamburger patties by crushing a ball of meat in the cook's armpit. It hadn't been that bad at O'Hare's, but the soup had come in frozen bricks.

Annie, her ex-husband, and the main cook, Alice, became yet another family to me. Annie's ex would ladle any leftover homemade soup into old sour cream containers for me at the end of my shift. Alice paid me to clean her apartment once a week, which usually entailed throwing out empty bottles of vodka from her bedroom and scrubbing exploded pop off the freezer walls. And Annie would school me on how to have a happy life, a message along the lines of "You have to go after what you want. No one will do it for you."

At the end of each shift, I'd mop the floor, hands wrinkled and pink, clothes damp and smelling of old, wet food, and compose more poetry. My head was full of words. My heart, full of dreams. Mainly of going to college, up north, to one of those places where the trees were older than the ivy-covered buildings. Where other people with words and dreams like mine would be. Where I might discover who I really was, who I could be.

I finished my junior year of high school and moved into an apartment with Doug. I was trying to embrace this story I found myself in. Trying to imagine myself in this future. I'd finish school. Work at Annie's. Maybe enroll in the community college. That maybe. I knew in my heart what maybe meant. But I tried, nonetheless.

My mother took me shopping at Sears with a new credit card. It was the first time I remembered shopping in a real store with her. She seemed proud of being able to do that. We hadn't been getting along the last several months, one of the reasons that prompted my moving out. Rather, I hadn't been getting along well with her. I yelled at her a lot. For talking too loud. For waking me up too early in the morning. For being a lousy parent. I hated how many times I made her cry. I'd wonder later if I was just being a typical hormonal teenage girl, but at the time I felt wretched. Who yells at their mentally ill mother?

At any rate, she took me shopping, and I bought a dark purple silk nightgown. It was gorgeous. I had never owned anything like it. I felt grown up in it. I felt sexy. I thought it would be the outfit of my new life. I would be a good woman to my good man. I would learn to make lasagna like his mother. I would learn to keep his socks white. I would learn to want what I had and not all those other things.

A few weeks after Doug and I moved into our new apartment, I headed to Ohio for a summer visit by myself. I didn't know yet that I would be leaving for good soon. I had every intention of returning to and staying in Florida after visiting my father and Nancy. Of finishing school, continuing to work at Annie's, maybe (never) going to community college.

While in Ohio, I visited Erica, who had moved to Akron with her father the previous year. It was at her house I met yet another boy. This boy was a friend of my friend's boyfriend. One night I got drunk and slept with him. This boy drove a Chevelle and had a smooth, muscular ass. There was nothing mythic about him. But having sex with him was one of the catalysts for making the choice I would make in a few weeks' time. It was the kind of small but pivotal experience my mother must have had before she decided to move south. I didn't know what hers was. Mine was sex with this boy.

He was my age. That was a big thing to me. Fucking him on a bare mattress in the loft of an abandoned barn on a cool Ohio summer night while crickets chirped over the car radio down below felt right. It felt normal. It seemed like something any typical American 17-year-old girl might do. Maybe it was Tom Petty singing on that car radio about his American girl, his voice drifting up into the loft and into my subconscious, mingling with our honest, heavy teenage breathing. Was that the moment my wanting something else tipped over into a willingness to make it happen?

Like my mother over a decade before, I left a man because I didn't want the life I thought fate would have afforded us. I was 17. He was 21. In our apartment, he had built me a shelf to hold the things I held most dear. He didn't share my love of books, but he respected it. I had no doubt he loved me. Wasn't that what every girl dreamed of? Someone to love her. As I would write in an autobiographical short story years later, I didn't know why it wasn't enough for me.

Unlike when my mother left my father, no one thought I was crazy for leaving. Not even Doug, who I was leaving behind. He was surprised but not surprised. He knew, like everyone else in my life, that I had what was called potential. When I told Heather about moving to Ohio, she said, "I knew you'd be the one to get out." She was pregnant with her first baby at the time, and she blew her cigarette smoke politely away from me after each drag. My sister's first husband would write me years later in a letter: "We got out and we know why." In high school, my 10th grade history teacher had told another teacher to watch out for me. "She's a thinker. She's going places."

In 1989, I was going someplace. I was going to Ohio, to live with my father and Nancy. In the days before I left Doug, my song was The Guess Who's "No Time." I had no time left for

Doug. No time left for Joseph. I had found myself some wings. The feeling: a simultaneous pushing and pulling behind the breastbone. Distant roads were calling me, and I couldn't wait— though for what, I had absolutely no idea.

I couldn't remember what my sister said or did when I told her I was leaving. She would've been 20 when I left. Her first baby, my niece, would've been nearly a year old. My sister was deep into a religious cult by then, no longer angry or feisty or bad; instead, she was eerily polite and did strange things, like try to exorcise my cat when it got leukemia.

I broke the news to Joseph in person that I was leaving. The memory of it was clearer than most of my memories. I had never been in his house before. We sat on his bed, and I tried to tell him what he meant to me, but I had no voice. Just the summer before, we could sit and stare into each other's eyes for hours, somehow saying everything we needed to say without having to say a word. On this day, though, we looked anywhere else and talked of easier things. Where I'd go to finish high school. What I would do with my car. Where I thought I'd go to college. I gave him my childhood teddy bear, and we both cried then, knowing the significance. Our shared favorite novel, "The Hotel New Hampshire," insisted that all one needed in life was a good, smart bear. It was what I had always called Joseph. Before I left, I stood on my tiptoes to hug him. "You're so tall," I said, and felt my knees weaken at the first, and what I believed would be the last, touch of his body against mine.

The night I broke the news to my mother and Tom I was going to live with my father, Doug sat on my mother's piano bench trying to keep himself together. I had told him earlier, though I couldn't recall when or how or where. It had to have hurt like hell. Doug had shaved off his mustache, and the fact that he looked so different without that scrap of facial hair made it easier for me to stick to my plan. But I could still see in his face that I was breaking his heart. I was going anyway. I could also see he was proud of me. It almost made me want to stay.

What had my mother seen in my father's face as she pulled out of the driveway? It was beyond a hard question. It was simply unaskable.

"I'll be going to college," I told them, sounding so sure of myself. So sure of everything. The only thing I was sure of was what I didn't want.

I didn't want to stay and live with Doug.

I didn't want to stay and break up with Doug.

I didn't even want to stay and be with Joseph.

I didn't want to stay.

There was only one choice left.

It seemed my adventure was chosen purely by default. But default implies reversion, a reset. I felt like I was venturing out rather than back. It was as though I were 10 years old again gripping the wrought iron "W" at my grandparents' Windsor Manor condo, only this time, I would move for real. Forward, beyond, captain of my own ship, in search of my own destiny.

And yet, I was going back. Pushed by winds of veiled design, back to my father who, for all his faults, never hesitated to say yes when I had asked to come ... home?

Seven:

1990 to 1994, College

Philosophy Notes

My doodling started in college, maybe to capture the things I felt but could not yet express.

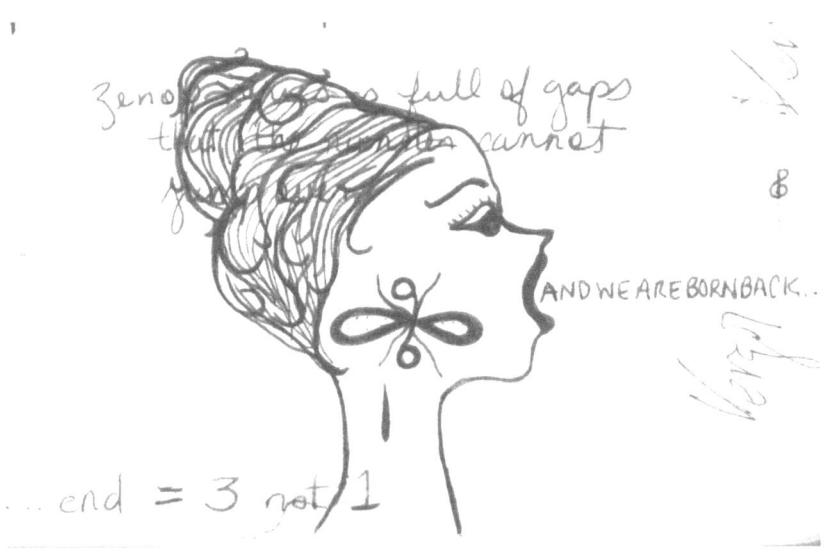

Even 25 years later, I would struggle to find the words. All I could do was try to conjure the feelings and describe them as best I could. The hand in the flour canister, soft and safe; the simultaneous push and pull behind the breastbone. Breathlessness. Exhilaration. Freedom.

I could be anything.

I wanted to be someone I couldn't even describe. But I could feel her.

When I looked at the girl in this doodle, I saw the girl I had wanted to become. Confident and sure of voice. Optimistic and open-eyed. I wanted to be borne back to that time when everything was right with my world, to move toward what I was meant to be. Reclaim what was supposed to be mine. Could I ever get there? Or, as in Zeno's paradox, would my destination always be just beyond reach? I was determined to press on.

I Could Be Anything

The guy from my Ancient Greek class was from Vancouver, British Columbia, which may as well have been Europe to me. He was a sophomore with wiry hair and eyeglasses that would remind me later of a Russian revolutionary. As a college freshman, I was not yet familiar with Russian revolutionaries and their style of eyewear. I was unfamiliar with many things.

"It's pronounced Ca-moo," he said. We were walking to the store so I could buy a pack of Camels (Marlboros being so high school). I was telling him what books I had read, trying to be impressive.

"Are you sure?" I had never heard the name out loud.

"It's French." Then he laughed. "You are so cute." He also thought it was cute that I thought I was madly in love with a high school boy all the way in Florida. "That is so bourgeois," he said, when I told him we were engaged to be married. I wanted to tell him it wasn't at all like what he thought—it was like what I thought—but I wasn't exactly sure what "bourgeois" meant.

Joseph, the boy all the way in Florida who I thought I was madly in love with, thought I was fucking the guy from my Ancient Greek class. I was not. Sure, I had had sex with a few men during my senior year of high school in Ohio, but that was well before Joseph's proposal. And as a single 17-year-old, when a man wanted to have sex with me, I thought it was my job to do so. What was I supposed to have done? Said no? I hadn't taken that class yet.

Joseph may have proposed before he flew up from Florida to be my date for senior prom, and I took his virginity that night at the Red Roof Inn. Or it may have been after. He popped the actual question in a letter. "Amanda Irene Hoyt, will you marry me?" I shrieked in the dining room of my father's house when I read it, my father calling from upstairs, "What the hell's the matter?"

That summer, Joseph gave me a ring—on bended knee, no less—when he and two of his friends drove up to visit. I wrote poetry about it: "So this is where our heartache ends and where our fairy tale begins." But as the days grew into weeks, I began to wonder if I'd been kidding myself. There I was in college dreaming up adventures that in no way included him, while he was down in Florida in college and becoming, I worried, an alcoholic. No matter how many postcards I sent him with carefully penned, badly composed inspirational haiku, I would not be able to alter the course he was on, that we were on.

Like many female undergrads, I read "The Bell Jar" and felt a stereotypical, albeit sincere, kinship with Esther Greenwood. While I read of Esther trying to slog through "Ulysses," I made grandiose plans to deconstruct the "Choose Your Own Adventure" books of my youth. No matter that I had no idea what deconstructionism was. It was one of those big new words that gave me that push-pull feeling behind my breastbone.

I could be anything.

I could be a scholar. Sitting under a tree on the lawn of Austin Manor, the college's then intergenerational apartment building, I pored over a thick volume of Nietzsche for my Modern Temper class, learning about the opposing tempers of the Appollonian and the Dionysian, soaking up those new and magical words, wanting to know, to understand, everything. I could see a future where I shared my thoughts with other people who cared about such things. I would wear tweed blazers with long skirts, my hair in a messy, effortless bun. I'd have glasses I could take off and put back on to make my clever points. I'd live in a small university town just like that one and invest in a couple of cats. I'd drink tea in the evenings while I read books or student papers. I would be content.

Or I could be a protégé. A partial scholarship recipient, mentored briefly by a young man and elderly woman, both residents in Austin Manor, I felt like Esther Greenwood, bursting with potential. Maybe those people, this young man and elderly woman, could help transform me into one of those girls who came from out east. One who owned sweater sets and still had her virginity. Maybe they could teach me what a tea sandwich was and which fork to use first at fancy dinners. Maybe I could wear opaque tights beneath calf-length skirts and keep my loafers unscuffed. Maybe I'd end up in New York City working in a publishing house.

Or I could be a wise soul. During a welcome weekend, when I gathered with other freshmen at a camp outside of Delaware, Ohio, that was close to my college campus, I approached a table in the dining tent with coffee set out next to a sign that said "For Counselors Only." I had hesitated before pouring a cup. I met a girl who was also wearing a Doors T-shirt. We chatted about our shared interests. Something about her made me feel at ease, comfortable in my own skin. She became a good friend and told me that when she met me she thought I was very wise. Yes, I thought. I could be very wise. I could be that person people come to for help. I could wear cardigans with deep pockets and let my hair flow long. I could learn to transform pain into healing.

Or I could be a poet. I spent Saturday nights at the coffeehouse in the basement of Stuyvesant Hall drinking cups of hot tea and chain-smoking Camels. I didn't own any clothes that said "poet," so who knows what I was wearing. Probably the same army-green pants and beige henley belted at the waist I'd been wearing since high school. Maybe old jeans and thrift store flannel. I wasn't wearing a beret, I was much too shy for that. I wanted to share my words during open mic but was certain my words were stupid. I gave up on words and took up doodling, still believing down deep that one day my words could be good enough. And once they were, I'd wear whatever I wanted and people would listen to what I had to say.

In no fantasy was I someone's fiancé, let alone wife. Yet, I wore the ring Joseph had given me, telling everyone how much in love we were. I was still a girl who believed in love. No one asked about our future. Would I move back to Florida? Would he move here to Ohio? What about kids? Our story—regardless of the ring, the engagement—would not get far enough along to warrant such choices.

At the end of October 1990, just months into my new life as a college co-ed, Joseph and I broke up. It was the day of my mother's wedding to Tom Mayle, and I was in Florida for the occasion, staying with Joseph because my mother had a friend living in the second bedroom at the duplex on Skyline Boulevard, and I wasn't about to sleep on one of those damn sectionals. Joseph and I had had a fight earlier that morning. He accused me of being a cheater, and I accused him of being an alcoholic. It didn't help that I was sporting a bad perm and that he insisted on wearing a full-length black leather duster. Even accounting for the style of the day, neither of us could have been more awkward or ridiculous in our own skins if we had tried. We were both apparently going through a phase, both trying to figure out who we were. It seemed we were getting closer to not being anything to the other. Before we left his house to drive to the wedding, I took the ring off my finger and put it on a chain around my neck. It was supposed to be symbolic of who knows what. The stone would leave small marks on my chest well into the new year.

At the ceremony, Joseph and I took seats in the back, the space between us charged in a way that was no longer positive. I was careful not to let my arm brush against his, or to let our knees knock. I held my breath and tried not to cry.

To this day, I am ashamed of what happened next. I have to remind myself that I was an 18-year-old kid who was on the verge of breaking up with a boy she once thought she was madly in love with. The tension was unbearable. Was it any wonder I began to laugh hysterically? I did, as soon as I caught a glimpse of my mother's expression up on the altar. She looked absolutely gone, the way she used to look when she sat in the rocker at night medicated out of her head trying to eat Doritos. We always laughed. Forgive me, I did.

A photo of my mother was snapped after the ceremony. For better or worse, this was the woman I laughed at, the woman I remembered, the woman I knew. My shadow mother. The one who lurked outside my bedroom door. The one who paced and smoked and stared. The one whose face was like stone. The one who always seemed never there.

What was she thinking the moment the photo was taken? Did she know I had been laughing on possibly the happiest day of her life? How could I ever make up for that?

Doug sent me a single rose for Valentine's Day during my freshman year. I must've been at my father's house over a long weekend because by the time I checked my campus mailbox, the flower had turned black and crispy. I took it as a symbol of what I had done to him, done to us. I had taken this beautiful love he had for me and let it die. I had also let the love Joseph and I had die. Surely, I would be punished. I waited fearfully for what fate would befall me, even as I continued to dream of what good things the future might hold.

I sent back to Joseph the ring he had given me, and our fairy tale officially ended. I took to taking four showers a day because it was the only private place to cry. I also took to torturing myself with the journal my mother had sent me as a gift. She meant, I was sure, for it to be a nice thing. Instead, I used it to apologize to the world that I was alive, taking up space, making mistakes, failing to be the person I felt I could be.

I could be anything.

I had become a breaker of hearts.

Doug and Joseph had become my father, left behind, abandoned, forgotten. This meant, according to my skewed emotional calculus, that I was my mother—the one who left and went crazy as punishment for her selfishness, for her dream of a better life, for daring to choose her own adventure.

My great adventure, leaving Doug, had led me right back to the same worn course of my parents' story. I had managed to escape the fate of marrying someone I did not love but had walked right into the scenario where I had become the cheater and the leaver, both. I would have to pay for my transgression, just as my mother had paid for hers.

The dreams began around that time. They were almost always violent, sexual, vivid. I saw them as my lot to suffer, but I also interpreted them as transformative. The shedding of old ways, the old me. I was determined to become a person I could be proud of. A person who didn't cower in anxiety. Who spoke her mind. Who knew what words to say and when and to whom. A person who would not take what she perceived as the easy way out by slipping into the waiting rutted roles of either her mother or her father. I wanted to be worthy. I wanted to be a person realized, not just wished for.

I dreamed of a dead baby, wet and bloated, floating in the toilet. What had it meant? I believed it represented the depressed self I wanted to reject. And the child I dreamed of—my reflection stepping out from a mirror—that I beat to a pulp until her skull cracked and her bones gave, crying about what I was doing as I was doing it, saying, "is that better, sweetie?" over and over until the child's eyes were full of blood and her teeth were red and her breath came out a hiss? A symbol of the strong emotions I felt about my time of personal change. And the near-nightly rapes, the murderous sex, the fighting back for my life? All symbols of a self's destruction and subsequent creation.

Could they have meant something else, those dreams? Could they have meant I was getting closer to my mother's illness, paying the price for my daring adventure? Did part of me feel that to get to the person I wanted to be, I would have to go through my mother's world of isolation and darkness? I was OK with that. If there was a price to pay, I was ready and willing to settle up. But would I be able to?

"I think I'm going crazy," I told a friend one night in the dorm kitchen while we made Velveeta shells and cheese. I bowed my face over the microwaved bowl of macaroni, letting the steam surround me. I was both embarrassed and ashamed of my confession.

"I don't think I'm smart enough to go crazy," she replied.

I heard more than that. I heard: "And neither are you."

When I finally called my father to tell him I thought I was depressed, he told me his problem was he always tried to please everyone and maybe that was my problem, too. I didn't think it was, but I appreciated his sober stab at honesty.

He sent me to a doctor who didn't do anything at all. What was there to do, really? I was showering (a lot) and getting straight As. Obviously, there wasn't anything wrong with me. I was being silly and dramatic, a young girl nursing her first broken heart. What the doctor didn't know was how many broken hearts I was trying to nurse: mine, Doug's, Joseph's, my mother's, my father's. The weight of my perceived responsibility was crippling.

I imagined my young self driving home from that doctor's appointment with Leonard Cohen in my tape deck. Yet another copy of one of my father's albums. It could have been "Teachers" playing, a song about suffering and everything it might make of us.

By the spring of my sophomore year of college, I had gotten over the depression and guilt triggered by my failed fairy tale and doomed legacy. I was growing my armpit hair and in love with a girl, trying that on for size. But it didn't fit, and I knew it. I was still waiting for something else. I was done looking back. I wanted an adventure that was all my own, not some rehash of a time gone past.

I wanted, I think, something bad to happen—to me. My father was never an abusive drunk, my mother never a raving lunatic. I got depressed but never thought about putting my head in an oven. Nothing bad had ever happened to me. Why would I want that? To prove myself. Prove what? And to whom? I wanted to be tested, to see what I was made of. To see if I could be worthy of the image I had of myself.

I had no journals from my freshman and sophomore years—I burned them all after I graduated. I couldn't imagine what I thought so mortifying about them that I felt I had to incinerate them; I'd held onto more incriminating things. Perhaps it wasn't embarrassment that drove them to the fire. Maybe it was part of my transformation. I found other proof, though: a typed journal starting in the spring of 1993, my junior year. There was an entry from May 13: "There are so many things I'm tired of being. Tired of being weak mainly. Frightened, worried, lonely, broody and sad." A few days later, this: "I need to let go of a lot of things. Old friends. Old me. My parents. Last year."

My memory served. I was ready for another, even bigger, change.

"Meet Stephen S." was what I wrote on the to-do page of my annual planner at the beginning of my junior year in the fall of 1992, almost as if I had beckoned him. But no, it was my classics professor who encouraged me to reach out to him. We were his two best students—Stephen in Latin, me in Ancient Greek—and he wanted us to work on a newsletter together for the department, "The Janus." How fitting. The two-faced god of beginnings and endings, of transitions.

I had seen Stephen around campus the previous year on many occasions. I had seen him reading and walking at the same time, his head bobbing to the heavy-sounding music coming out of the headphones of his Discman. I had seen him playing guitar in his punk rock band at the coffeehouse in Stuyvesant Hall. I had seen him in some classes we shared. And I had seen him after dinner outside one of the dining halls with his three band mates and a dark-haired girl of pale, unconventional beauty who would often be sitting on his lap. These four were the only people Stephen talked to as far as I could tell. He struck me as sullen yet sophisticated, the kind of person who couldn't be bothered with silly things.

The day Stephen and I met, I sat outside Phillips Hall waiting for my history of ancient philosophy class to start. I was smoking a cigarette. I had recently kissed my best girlfriend and had done other things with her that had made me feel embarrassed, ashamed and brave all at once. Just shy of 20, I was a super fantastic flake with little sense of myself. I was searching for God knows what, and Stephen seemed to have it. There he was standing in front of me, his book closed and his headphones around his neck, giving a silly thing like me the time of day. I hoped I looked a great deal less nervous than I felt.

"I know something about you I'm not supposed to know," he said.

Could he possibly have known what I had done with my best girlfriend?

"You're living illegally off campus."

I exhaled and wondered if Stephen thought the cigarette that I was smoking made me look sophisticated. In both my old and current circles, smoking was cool. But I sensed Stephen was not part of any such circles. The cigarette seemed only to add to my overall silliness, and I regretted him catching me smoking it.

I confessed to him that I was indeed living illegally off campus. I was on the top floor of a dilapidated duplex with my best friend and a guy from Malaysia.

"Don't worry," he said. "I won't tell."

It was an early autumn afternoon and the weather was still hot. I was suddenly conscious of the hair under my arms, and I wished I had sleeves on my shirt. I was also conscious of the pungent but not unpleasant smell that was coming from Stephen. A glandular smell, of sweat and sebum, like the smell under your nails after you scratch your head. He was not a cute guy. He was a big, sweaty guy with a shock of bangs falling over a broad forehead that always made me think of the word Teutonic. He had somewhat crooked teeth and fleshy lips, which made for a nice smile. He carried himself like he owned the world but would never be stingy with it as long as he deemed you worthy. From the moment I met him, I wanted to be worthy.

Stephen was the first person to say mean things to me on purpose. "You're really too short for me," he told me several weeks later. We were dating by then, which for us translated into having a lot of sex and taking long walks at night. I had shaved my armpits and drastically reduced my smoking. I began distancing myself from all my friends, whom Stephen hated. They hated him right back and were exasperated with me. I didn't care. I was trying hard to be whatever it was Stephen wanted so he would stay around and show me how to walk through the world the way he did, with confidence and poise and self-respect.

Even years later, well into our marriage, I thought he held the key for what I was after. In a journal from 1997, I wrote about meeting him at college: "Here was a person who was connected to the world. He was confident and communicative. He always seemed to know what to do and say. Here was someone who had it all figured out." What had he figured out? I jotted that down in that '97 journal too: "Our lives are not predetermined, cookie-cut, laid in stone. It is our responsibility to create our lives and bring meaning to that life." My younger self was right about our responsibility to bring meaning to our lives. The gathering of ephemera, for instance—what was it but an attempt to bring meaning to my life? But I would come to believe very much in the role of fate and its uncanny knack of anticipating the choices we make.

Whether it was my choice or my fate to hitch my wagon to Stephen's star, I did, willingly. Even when he told me he still loved the pale, dark-haired girl of unconventional beauty, I wasn't deterred. He said he never wanted to lie to me. I had never met anyone so committed to honesty, at least not anyone sober. I had lived too long with secrets. Too long with no one saying what they meant, meaning what they said. I found it refreshing to know exactly how things stood.

Sometimes his honesty hurt. One night as I flipped through an old photo album with him, I said something self-conscious about an old picture of me—"Look how cute I was!"—or something to that effect. "Your vanity sickens me," he said and got up and left. On another occasion, I showed up at his dorm room and said something off-hand about the music he was listening to. Again, I was self-conscious, trying to be light and funny. "What is that? Devil music?" But instead, I offended him. He gave me the silent treatment for a good 40 minutes. I was so afraid to open my mouth again. Afraid to move. Afraid to breathe. He went about his evening as though I weren't even in the room, and I felt myself shrink further and further into nothingness.

I felt that this new annihilation was necessary. This was the adventure I had been seeking. If I could stand it, I would learn what I wanted to know. Could become who I wanted to become.

Months later, when he told me he thought he was falling in love with me, I didn't want to lie, either. I told him I didn't think I loved him as much as he loved me. He did not find my commitment to honesty refreshing. He cried. He got angry. He accused me of not knowing what love was. I cried too. I got scared he would leave. I told him he was right. I didn't know what I was saying. Of course, I loved him.

In my most secret place, I knew I didn't love him, but I didn't care. I was on a mission. I didn't want to be the flaky, silly girl with no sense of herself or of her place in the world.

A week after graduation, I married him.

We got married on a Thursday, May 12, 1994. It was a hasty wedding and we both had other plans for the weekend. He was going to Graceland with a friend, and I was headed out to visit my sister who was living in South Dakota. When I told her I was married, she looked reasonably shocked and asked me about him. "He's kind of an asshole," I told her.

What did that make me? What kind of girl marries a guy who's kind of an asshole? It was nobody I wanted to be. And yet, I felt I would have to be this girl to become the girl I felt I could be.

This was the version of my story I wanted to believe. That I was a bold, daring girl on a mission to find herself. It was partly true. I did believe Stephen possessed some quality that would help me figure out who I was, who I could become. There was the proof I found in that 1997 journal. But even earlier than that, I believed it. Four years earlier, I had written: "Finally a person to get in my face. To force me to really look at myself. To question my wants, needs, etc. Someone to bring me out of me."

The other part of the truth, though, was that I was lost. My bold move to Ohio had not led me home, and though college was an amazing experience, by the time I met Stephen I had no idea who I was or where I was going, and there was nowhere to go back to. Not to my father, who by that time had made his shattering confession about his love for Callie Smith. Not to my mother, who by that time had moved to Colorado with her new husband. And not to my sister, who by that time was in a new state, as well, knee-deep in Jesus. I was once again, perhaps more than ever before, adrift.

And all I knew, again, was what I didn't want. I didn't want to be my father, constantly striving for someone else's idea of success. I didn't want to be my mother, a ghost in my own life. I was ready and willing for fate to take me anywhere it chose. And in fate's absence, I was willing to let someone like Stephen choose my fate for me.

Stephen once said he believed I could be anything that he wanted me to be. How right he was. He would ask me to be many things in the next 10 years. He would not want me to be—demand, actually, that I not be—either one of my parents. At that time in my life, with the girl I wanted to be so close I could feel her, that was good enough for me.

The story of our 10-year marriage is another story, for another time. Suffice it to say I was tested. I was surprised. There were many adventures. "We had an incredible life together, didn't we?" Stephen had asked in a letter right after our divorce. Yes, we had. During those years with him, I had been an alarm system installer, a private investigator, a real estate investor, a loan processor, a loan closer, a stripper, an adult movie actress, a nude model, a small business owner and a graduate student. I had learned how malleable and reckless and fearful I was. How tolerant and intolerable. How eager and accommodating. How determined. I went bankrupt financially and morally and, thanks to Stephen's penchant for shared extramarital activities, racked up a list of sexual partners that would've impressed my mother. I became what Stephen considered most worthy: tough. "Too tough to put up with the likes of me?" he asked in that same letter.

I became both my parents, too. I climbed my own ladder of what I deemed success until there was nowhere to go but down. And in Stephen's shadow, I became such a ghost I could barely even see myself.

A few years into our marriage, Stephen told me he could get anyone to do what I did for him—rub his back and calves, read to him in the tub, keep him company on long walks, listen to him pontificate. "I could get a monkey," he said. And I smiled and danced, tried to be the best monkey I could be, still believing that eventually I would find what I was looking for—me.

Stephen wasn't always mean. He was often, but not always. Sometimes he was very funny. Usually at my expense, but still, funny. Wasn't it hilarious when he kicked me out of the car in Columbus during a snowstorm and I had to beg a cab driver to take me the 40-some miles to Marion on my last few dollars?

"You really made it home?!" he said, laughing from the tub.

That's how I will forever remember Stephen, sitting in a tub with a mutilated book propped on his hairy stomach. He always ripped the pages out as he read them. He devoured books like he damn near devoured me. By the time he was done with me, there was barely anything left.

But there was enough.

Eight:
Endings

Then Those Stones

In 2009, five years after my divorce from Stephen, when I was about a year into practice as a psychiatric nurse practitioner, an angry patient said to me, "I don't know what your problem is. Maybe your mother had schizophrenia and you're trying to save the world because you feel bad about the way you treated her."

Her words struck swift and cut deep, exposing the guilt I had bourne for nearly a decade since my mother's death.

I did feel bad about the way I had treated my mother. I had treated her like she was a lost cause. "My mother had a breakdown," I had said over and over. In the dominating narrative of my life thus far, my mother was broken, and I never had faith she could be put back together again. Only now did I realize she wasn't nearly as damaged as I thought. In the years between her breakdown and her death, she made friends, married a good man and fulfilled a lifelong dream of moving to Colorado. She regretted parts of her past, had hopes for the future, and loved and struggled like any other person did. But I hadn't seen her as a person. I hadn't seen her. I had been blinded by her illness.

No, not blinded. Blinded relieved me of agency. I had made a choice. How many times had I described her as crazy, nuts, no longer my mother? I hadn't been blinded; I had been blind.

I didn't know if it was true, that I treated my mother badly. My sister didn't think so. Whenever I asked her, she always reminded me that she was the one who stole our mother's car and slapped her and once threw a glass of milk in her face. And stabbed her.

I mined my mother's journals. She left behind 15, spanning the time between Apr. 30, 1996, to two days before her death, on May 30, 2000. I found things she wrote about my sister. She didn't trust her. She felt judged by her. She never forgave her for the things she did, though I didn't find anything about a stabbing. She also wrote that she was proud of my sister. And impressed by how well-behaved her children were.

What I really wanted to know was what my mother thought of me. Had she thought I treated her badly? Had she loved me?

I visited her in Colorado for the first time on the first day of 1998. I read the entries in her journal, which was how I knew the date. What my mother didn't write about that visit was how she had the spare bedroom prepared for me with clean sheets and blankets on the bed, and on the side table a dish of prayer stones with words like "Peace," "Love" and "Joy" engraved on each. She stood in the doorway looking toward but not at me as I sat on the bed and gathered the stones in my hand. Each one a gift I didn't feel I deserved to receive. Each one a gift I didn't feel she deserved to give.

It had been three years since I had seen my mother. Longer even since I had really seen her. I couldn't help thinking of everything we had lost, everything she had missed. It wasn't fair to blame her, but I blamed her anyway. Blamed her for everything she did—the smoking, the pacing, the staring, the talking too loud when she did talk. And everything she didn't do—act like a normal mother, prepare me for the world, make sense, be unembarrassing.

But then those stones.

In the silence that hung between us, not as annihilating, but still palpable, painful, I imagined her choosing those stones. Finding a dish to hold them. Placing them on the table in the room she prepared especially for me. I blinked hard against tears threatening to spill. I couldn't speak. In my throat there were other stones, one word on all of them: Sorrow. Sorrow was confusing. It was a soft word that hurt.

If my mother felt the sorrow that day, she didn't write about it. She didn't write about a lot of things. Most of her journal entries involved the day-to-day minutiae of her life: how many cups of coffee she drank; how many aspirin she took; how many hours of sleep she got; what chores she managed to do; what she had for dinner. Quotidian. She would have liked that word, though the word she used to describe her entries was mundane. My mother loved words, as I love words. In her pages I came across vociferous, ambulate, coif and gullet. According to one entry, I once caused her to contemplate the word puissant. I had no recollection of this at all; I didn't even know what that word meant. I had to look it up.

Jul. 5, 1998. There was nothing special about the date, only that it was a date on which my mother and I both wrote journal entries. I compared the two, looking for anything that might help answer the hard questions I had about love and hurt and sorrow.

In the summer of 1998, my mother was documenting her days and slowly turning into a recluse. I, meanwhile, was dancing nude six days a week at a strip club and contemplating graduate school. We were both married; she to Tom, me to Stephen. She may have written her entry at the kitchen table, possibly naked, as she liked to be naked, a cigarette burning in the ashtray. I was at the club where I was working, waiting for my turn to dance, writing by the light above the pool table, the music thumping around me. My mother wrote her mundane details while I wrote a list of words from a book I was reading. The list of words I did not know was long: evanescent, abstruse, opined, imbued, suffused, sacrosanct, bruja, anathema, curandera, refractory. Puissant was not on the list, nor could I find it on any list in any of my other journals. The word remained a mystery.

I made a new list.

Things my mother thought about me (as discovered in her journals):

I had a lot to learn.

I was not an ingrate.

I was at the top of the list of people who had hurt her the most.

I was one of her most trusted friends.

I had potential with learning to play the piano.

I was a go-getter.

I was an atheistic person.

I would make a lousy mother.

I was impressed by mountains.

I didn't write often enough.

I didn't call often enough.

I was self-actualized.

I was aggressive.

I was a dynamo.

I did not disapprove of her tattoo.

I once caused her to contemplate the word puissant.

I wanted to be a student the rest of my life.

I was one of her hopes for the future.

I was her love child and she treasured me.

I once covered her with a blanket.

Over 20 items I'd mined and still I struggled to come up with a clear sense of who she thought I was.

Was. I was no longer the same person I had been at any time in my past. And yet, I wasn't too terribly different. I felt I had been borne back to the person I was on the road to becoming before my mother's illness hit. I felt I had been put back together. Missing pieces found and repaired. Hurts healed.

I went to work at the club the night after she died. I told the girls and my manager and even one of my regulars (a guy who went by Daniel and who liked me to rub my bare feet on his bald head during private shows). Everybody hugged me and a few girls cried. I felt numb. I had cried in the morning when my stepfather called to give me the news, and later when I went to the library with Stephen, and again when I spoke to my father and Nancy and some old friends from Florida. But at the club that night, I didn't feel anything. My mother died. The sentence went through my mind and out my mouth all night. But it was just a statement, void of emotion. I was, I would later learn, in the first stage of grief: denial. Like so much else when it came to my mother, I was choosing to not see the grabby roots exposed beneath my feet. Keep moving. Keep working. Keep dancing. Nothing to feel here. I should feel something. My mother died.

Daniel asked me what she died of, and I told him about how she had become a morbidly obese recluse. "Her heart blew," I told him. "And she was crazy."

I couldn't remember what I danced to, but given my desire—more a feeling of obligation—to feel something, I likely played mournful songs like the Counting Crows' "Round Here" and Pink Floyd's "Wish You Were Here." Both about crazy people—crazy people who were, despite the song titles, no longer here. They were songs my mother might have liked. I would've liked to have known what it was I was supposed to feel and I would've liked to have felt it. The music may have helped.

After one set, I sat with Daniel and ate a Balance Bar. "Is that your dinner?" he asked me.

"I've gotta watch my figure," I told him, playfully batting my eyelashes.

He looked at me sadly. "You know that won't bring her back, right?"

His comment made me angry, ashamed, confused. The chocolate stuck in my throat, and I finally felt something: I felt like I had been found out. What was I doing there? I should have been in Colorado. My mother had died.

Still, I went to work the next night. And the night after that. I did not go to Colorado, where my mother had lived, where she had died. My sister went. "It was the right thing to do," she told me when I called her to ask why she went and I didn't. "It would have been wretched not to go. I mean, I've been wretched, but not that wretched." She was quick to reassure. "It's not like you missed anything," she said, reminding me how there hadn't been any kind of memorial. My mother hadn't wanted a big to-do.

I watched the video of the Counting Crows' "Round Here." I was almost certain I danced to it that night of the day my mother died. In the video, there was a woman with flowing gray hair wearing a flowing white gown. She roamed the streets like a ghost, holding up a sign: "Nobody move and nobody gets hurt." Maybe I thought if I didn't make a move, my mother's death wouldn't hurt.

From my mother's journal, May 28, 2000, her last entry, two days before her death: "I started reading about reincarnation. From Christian, Jewish, Essene, Hindu and Buddhist points of view. The similarities are few. Each group practices dogma."

My mother may well have passed on to another life, but some part of her stuck around to haunt me. For months after her death, I had a recurring dream in which the phone would ring, and I would answer it and I'd hear my mother's voice: "Amy? This is your mother!" It was what she always said in real life, and in the dream I would feel the familiar guilty dread of having to talk to her mixed in with the desire to want to talk to her. In the dream, I'd soon remember that she was dead and would feel fear settle heavy on my chest as I imagined her reaching for me from beyond, coming for me, the roots that bind us like tendrils from some dark, cold place.

"She's dead!" I would slam down the phone, and wake up, my eyes wide and my chest tight. I'd turn toward Stephen and take comfort in what warmth I could draw from his sturdy, sleeping body. Sometimes, he'd wake up. "What's wrong?" And I'd turn around and nestle in, feel the weight of his arm as I clutched it close, feel the hair tickle my nose, his scent deep and a little sweet. She's dead, I would think, no longer afraid, already aching for one more annoying phone call.

By the end of summer, I was in a constant state of either uncontrollable tears or unprovoked rage. Not yet schooled in the ways of grief, I went to the student health women's clinic and told the woman I assumed was a doctor that my birth control pills were finally making me crazy.

"After all this time?" she asked innocently. I had only been on them half my life. "Anything new that might be causing your moods?"

"Well," I said, "My mother died a few months ago." I promptly burst into tears.

This woman I assumed was a doctor was a nurse practitioner. She sent me to counseling, to which I faithfully went, and a seed was planted among the grabby roots of grief.

Four years later, right after my divorce from Stephen, I would enroll in nursing school. Had I hoped to save someone like this woman had saved me? Or, like my patient would later insinuate, was I hoping to make amends for how I treated my mother? I wasn't sure. If nothing else, nursing offered a way to support myself after my divorce. It also offered the promise of comfortable shoes.

I flew to Colorado nine months after my mother's death, finally ready to bear the truth and relinquish any hope I may have had that we would ever be anywhere near normal. The mother who I had missed for the majority of my life was now missing for good. All that was left were fuzzy memories, bad feelings and a shameful sense of relief.

The visit was a blur. I stayed with Tom, and we ate one night at my mother's favorite Mexican restaurant. What would we have talked about? He had me look through things, though I couldn't recall what. Plans were made for him to pack some things up and send them to me, to my sister. After Tom went to bed, I snuggled with Scout, their dog, comforted by his warmth and sporadic sighs. I wondered if he had been by her side when she died. Had he seen death coming? Had he smelled it?

Before I left, Tom gathered up my mother's journals for me to take back to Ohio. He gave me a secondhand bag that had belonged to her. It was maroon and had Gloria Vanderbilt printed on the side, which made me think of Laura, my long-ago surrogate mother, and her purple swan smell. I packed the books in the bag; the 15 just fit. I walked through the airport with the bag slung over my shoulder. The weight of it hurt and threw me off balance. I half resented having to lug them all the way home. It didn't occur to me then what a gift she had left me.

Years later, when I sat down to read them, her intention became clear to me. In her first entry, on Apr. 30, 1996, when she was the same age as me at the time I first read it (48), she wrote: "Someday, I hope my girls will read my journals. Perhaps this simple legacy will benefit them."

Oddly, what would benefit me the most was my mother's autopsy report. I studied it looking for what I missed, what I failed to see, what I refused to see.

The details of the report comforted me. Everything was so black and white. So precise. Her heart, for example, weighed

560 grams. Her liver, 2,980 grams. Her right and left lungs, 580 and 540, respectively. Her brain, 1,280.

I wished I could have held her heart in my hands. Felt the weight of it. Or the lightness of it. It was half the weight of her brain, a sixth of her liver. That surprised me. I had always imagined hearts being heavy, especially hers.

The report spoke of ventricular hypertrophy, maximum focal stenosis, smooth and glistening pleural surfaces. It told me the color and size of her gallstones. It told me that her left ovary and appendix were absent. It told me her bony structures demonstrated their usual relationships.

It told me she was 5 feet 6 inches tall and weighed 290 pounds. That she appeared older than her reported age of 52 years. That she died wearing a purple nightgown with a floral print, her natural teeth in good repair. A small amount of black ink was present over her ventral fingertips. Over her right cheek was a raised, light brown mole. Over her left upper chest, a tattoo depicting a rose.

The report told me in complicated language that she died of heart trouble. There's no mention of depression or loneliness, bitterness or regret, but I knew she died of those, too.

The report told me she died alone on her couch on a Tuesday at 6:09 in the morning with no evidence of suicide or homicide. It told me her death was natural.

Above all, the report told me this: my mother was not a ghost. She was flesh and blood. Liver and brain. Heart and bone.

Mercy

Sometime between 1968 and 1969, somewhere in South Vietnam, a young Air Force staff sergeant went up in a helicopter with some other soldiers. They'd scored some beer and wanted to go to the beach for a little unsanctioned R&R. The soldiers didn't make it to the beach. The chopper was hit by enemy fire and started to go down. The young Air Force staff sergeant grabbed a chute and jumped.

"He was the only one to survive the crash," a good friend of my father's said of him at his memorial service nearly 50 years later, in May 2015. "He was captured by the Vietcong and held in a bamboo cage. He chewed his way out and roamed alone through the jungle, acting crazy when he came to villages so the people would keep their distance. He eventually made his way back to his base. He was a courageous man. A man of utmost character."

My sister and I sat in our places of honor in the front row, surrounded by people who questioned our right to sit there, stunned by what we were hearing. The story was a new one for us.

This was not the man we had known. Could we have been wrong about him all those years?

My sister and I didn't know any of that about our father when we chose to set our lives aside and share caretaking duties for him while he battled neck cancer in 2014. He was to us then what he had been for many years—estranged, vain, casually cruel, oblivious. He was a man who drank too much and gave too little. We also knew he was only like that with us, his daughters. To everyone else in his life—his friends, his colleagues, his bartenders—he was a warm, giving, sensitive soul who laughed as easily as he cried after a few glasses of his favorite "finest" red wine. My sister and I didn't drink, and we weren't impressed with money.

He may not have deserved the care my sister and I gave, but we deserved to do it. I wasn't sure if my father would have done it for us, though he did do it for my stepmother. He was by Nancy's side until her sad end, taken a year earlier at the young age of 57 by her hard-heart disease, amyloidosis. He was not, as I've said before, the kind of man to walk away.

Why did we do it? Put our lives on hold to care for a man who never gave enough? Maybe we knew that deep down our dear ol' dad was a good guy. Maybe we needed to believe he was a good guy. Maybe we needed to prove that we were as good as we believed ourselves to be.

Why ever we did it, it was the right thing to do. He was our father. We were his girls. Sure, he had close friends, even surrogate children who drank the right wine and owned the right shoes, drove the right cars, but we were family. And though our roots with our father were as faint and tenuous as telephone lines captured in the pictures from long ago, they grabbed nonetheless.

There wasn't even a discussion as I recall. Our father must've been getting a biopsy or a scope or a scan the day my sister and I sat alone in a waiting area of University Hospital in Cleveland. We had been given the news earlier: radiation five days a week, he would need to be driven to and fro, he'd need help at home. One of us dug a pen out of a purse and on a scrap piece of paper we drew a crude calendar and cut the weeks in half, alternating Wednesdays. My sister would take Sunday through Tuesday; I, Thursday through Saturday.

"It was easy-peasy," my sister told me when I called to make sure I got it right.

"That's how I remember it!" I said. I was always excited when our memories intersected because it provided much firmer footing than my memory alone.

Then she told me how she came across his IBM portrait earlier in the day, and we were both silent for a moment as we thought about who he was to us, who he wasn't.

"Do you think he deserved what we did for him?" I asked her. "I just wrote that he didn't."

"Sure, he did," she said. "We all get screwed up and turned around."

After I hung up, I sat and pondered my sister's capacity for love. Or was it denial? I couldn't decide.

My father joined the Air Force when he was 19 and, according to his Armed Forces discharge report (Form DD 214), he spent one year and two days in foreign service. Some would argue that because of his sacrifice in the Vietnam War, the Western world was saved from communism, thus allowing me the freedom to go to the fancy private college I attended and sit under a tree reading my fancy books, dreaming of all the adventures that awaited me, believing in all the things I could be. I get that, and I'm thankful for the opportunity my father afforded me. But the war and my father's part in it left another legacy—it was a good excuse for him to drink.

It was a well-worn narrative. Vietnam had been a horrific experience for tens of thousands of GIs, driving many toward self-destructive habits. Why would my father be any different? He rarely talked about the war, seemed even to go out of his way to distance himself from it, though in his basement stained glass workshop he'd hung that POW/MIA flag. Over the years, on the few occasions Nancy left us to sit alone, he'd steadily sip his wine and toss out random comments like crumbs, but never enough to help me find my way into the story. "I promised myself I'd never live like that again." "They'd give guys blood they knew had malaria in it." "They gave me a gun when I got there but I refused to use it." "When your mom was in that state hospital, I knew just how she felt." Or, he wouldn't say a thing but would simply close his eyes, purse his lips around his pipe stem, and sadly shake his head as though trying to scatter the images only he could see.

It was very likely my father could have beaten the cancer if he could have beaten the alcohol. Once Nancy died, though, he drank as though his life depended on it. Only when it was too late would he realize that his life depended on him not drinking.

Deep, though, was his denial. Once, when he and I met with an oncologist at University Hospital, the doctor asked him if he smoked, and my father shook his head. "Are you kidding me?" I said before I could contain myself. "Well, I just smoke a pipe," said my father, as though pipe smoking didn't count. The doctor assured him it did. A few minutes later when the doctor asked about alcohol, my father was about to lie again—he didn't consider "fine wine" a problem—when he caught my eye. I nodded my head at him theatrically and my father followed suit.

While my father received traditional radiation (five days a week as promised), he chose to do chemo and alternative treatments at a holistic clinic that my sister had found. The clinic was run by Mrs. Chung, a no-nonsense Korean nurse who treated brown rice like a sacrament and who believed in the augury of poop. A doctor ostensibly ran the clinic, but Mrs. Chung was the one in charge. By the end of the first week, she had my father on nearly 20 supplements, instructed him on how to self-administer a coffee enema, and cautioned him about drinking alcohol. To his credit, my father did everything Mrs. Chung told him to— except eat brown rice and not drink alcohol.

Even if my father had dried out before the start of 2015, who's to say what would have happened? By mid-March when he wrapped up his radiation and IV chemo, his ankles were swollen. Mrs. Chung stood over him and shook her head. "Low protein," she said. "You have to eat, Mr. Hoyt." Problem was, he could barely stand to eat or drink anything, not even his fine wine. The radiation had been scouring. "It's like having a bucket of hot sand poured down my throat," my father had said after several weeks of treatment, wincing as he spoke.

Mar. 20, 2015. I didn't need any artifacts to remind me of that date. It was the last day my father stood on his poor swollen feet. It was a Friday. I had been with him since Wednesday and wanted to drive home that evening. It had been a nightmare day. My father's stomach had swollen beyond reason, seemingly overnight, until he looked like a pregnant woman well past her due date. Mrs. Chung had inserted a feeding tube that afternoon so we could try to get some protein in him, but I knew even then it was more than just low protein. Though my specialty is psychiatry, I remembered enough from nursing school to recognize ascites, the accumulation of fluid in the abdominal cavity, a tell-tale sign of advanced liver failure.

The image of him waddling (my handsome and vain father, waddling!) into the Mansfield ER that afternoon to have the tube placement confirmed still haunted me. I should have had more sympathy for him, but he had been such an ass all day. Scolding me for driving too slow, too fast, for slamming the door of his Lexus. "You've been doing it for weeks now," he croaked. "I wish you'd be more careful." Jesus Christ! I just wanted to run.

When I finally got him home, I made arrangements for his younger brother to stay the night with him until my sister could get there the next morning. I could not recall why I was leaving that night and not staying over. Maybe it was panic on my part. Maybe not panic. It was whatever the word is for when you are so overwhelmed and sad and angry you can't see straight. Whatever the word, that's what I was that Friday night, standing in front of my bloated father with a tube dangling from his nose.

"Are you sure you won't stay?" he asked. "Just until tomorrow?"

"You'll be fine, Pops," I said, looking him straight in his soft blue eyes. I could see clear enough he was scared out of his mind. Still, all I could say was, "It's not like you're gonna die."

For most of my life I regretted how I treated my mother. I treated my father just as badly, if not worse, and it never bothered me a bit. Well, as I thought of that night in late March 2015, it bothered me. But that was an old narrative, that business about treating my parents badly. I realized that was not so much regret at how I behaved but a hard-to-name feeling that they were both disappointed in me. That I was something hoped for but never realized. A squirrely feeling of an unspoken obligation not fulfilled. What did they want from me? The question, an old haunt.

Tax Day 2015. Another date I could remember without effort. My father had spent the last three weeks in Parma Hospital having the fluid drained from his abdomen. Liters and liters and liters of fluid. Eventually, the fluid became loculated, meaning it was no longer free flowing, but a gelatinous goo stuck in the infected webby mesh of the peritoneal cavity. There was nothing more they could do. "I'm sorry I let it get this bad," he had said to me one day while we were in the hospital. "Do you think I still look good enough for an open casket?" he had said on another.

My sister and I arranged for him to be transferred to a skilled nursing facility in Columbus, closer to us. I drove him down in his Lexus, closing the passenger door gently after the attendant helped me settle my father in the front seat and an oxygen tank in the back. What did we say during that long ride? I know what I didn't say: "It's not like you're gonna die."

That mid-April day, in the courtyard of the skilled nursing facility, as we basked in the cool spring sunshine, my father in his wheelchair, me on a bench beside him, my father looked up into the chill blue sky and said, "I want this to be over."

I started to cry then, right in front of him. How many weeks had I been trying not to do that? I clarified that he was talking about wanting to die.

"Yes," he said.

I cried a little harder, but silently, my head instinctively lowering so no one would see how my bottom lip protruded out in a most stereotypical fashion when I'm sad. I was still able to talk at this point, my crying self neatly compartmentalized over there so my rational self could discuss his wanting to die over here. My emotions, I thought, were loculated. It was the wrong use of the word, but I found comfort in the sound of it, the idea of it, nonetheless.

He said he'd like his feeding tube removed. "They can't force feed me," he said in a soft, pained rasp, "can they?"

I shook my head. "You have a living will stating you don't want artificial means of survival. I think the feeding tube constitutes artificial means."

"How long would it take?"

"To die?" Again, I wanted to be clear.

He nodded.

I told him I didn't know; I didn't. Only later, when he was at the hospice facility, would I look it up and find "Survival Rules of Three": three minutes without oxygen; three days without water; three weeks without food.

My father, it would turn out, would last three weeks with no food or water.

"I'm not afraid of dying," he said. "It's better than this." By this he meant no longer being able to eat or drink anything (not even ice chips), getting his abdomen drained (that is, until the fluid had turned to goo), being completely and utterly reliant on others (on the nurses to relieve his pain, on the aides to bathe him, on my sister and me to find "Law and Order," "Blue Bloods" and "The Big Bang Theory" on TV, and to place cool wet washcloths on his forehead). And the most recent "this," having to wear a diaper because he no longer had the sensation of when he was having a bowel movement. Even if he did, he wasn't strong enough to negotiate a bedpan by himself.

I wiped my nose on the sleeve of my jacket and willed the tears to stay over there.

"Do you think they'll give me a pedicure?" my father asked, and I had to smile. I doubted we could get anything more than a podiatry consult.

The next night I arranged for my husband Aaron's niece, a salon owner, to stop by and give my father a mani and a pedi. When she was done, he gave her as enthusiastic a thumbs up as he could muster in his weakened, morphined state.

The worst part of my father telling me he wanted to die was having to tell my sister. Not that I thought she would be distraught by the news—my sister respected a person's wish to leave the world. In fact, when she saw an animal dead on the side of the road, she'd comment that it must've decided to "check out." My sister was able to appreciate the cycle of life and death and life long before I was. No, what I dreaded was revealing that he had talked to me about this biggest of choices, not to her, not to us. It exposed that wound I nursed my whole life—I was the favorite.

I had reveled in my status as much as I had regretted it. It had been an infliction and a gift.

One day, long after our father had died, I told my sister I had been thinking about how our relationship had been a complicated mix of rivalry and devotion. It was a phrase I'd been kicking around in my head for some time, not quite ready to put it on the page. I threw it out there to test its accuracy.

"I've never been in competition with you," she said, sounding offended.

I tried then to explain to her how I meant that I was always secretly happy to be the favorite but that I remained devoted to her. I got all mixed up and felt bad for bringing it up.

She seemed to know exactly what I was trying to say. "I know they loved you more than me," she said without any hint of self-pity. "I don't care."

"You used to. You used to hate me when we were kids."

I was thinking of a letter I had found that she wrote for a teacher the year our mother had her breakdown. "My main problem now," her 13-year-old self wrote, "is that I'm madly jealous of my little sister. Everyone loves her and treats me like dirt. I hope I get over it though."

"I didn't hate you," my sister said. "I just hated that everyone thought you were so great and that I was such a pain in the ass. But I was a pain in the ass, so it's OK."

We were silent for several minutes and in those minutes, I thought about telling her about our mother's journal entries, in which she wrote how she never trusted my sister and considered me her love child. But I held my tongue.

When the admitting nurse from the hospice facility asked my father if he had non-alcoholic or alcoholic cirrhosis, he said alcoholic without missing a beat before looking at my sister and me and adding, "I confess!"

In the week before he slipped into unconsciousness, he called in his closest friends to the hospice facility to say his goodbyes. Most cried, but my father wanted levity. "I'm holding court," he joked, "like the Pope." When his youngest brother came to say goodbye, he grew serious and warned him to stop drinking now if he didn't want to end up like him. My sister and I were permanent attendees. We took turns sleeping on the couch in his room, rubbing his feet with lavender and frankincense oil, fluffing his pillows, combing his hair.

My mother had died within minutes, and she had died alone. My father was taking his sweet time and was surrounded by his two girls who despite his sometimes shitty work as a father let him know he was loved up until the end.

Even more unlike my mother, who likely died not knowing that her girls loved her deeply, though sorrowfully, my father let us know he knew.

"I'm going to need a big box," he said just days before losing consciousness for good. My husband, Aaron, and I were at his bedside. Me, holding my father's hand. He had just apologized for waking up, for not being dead yet. His voice was as soft as smoke.

I felt Aaron's hand on my shoulder as I leaned in close to catch my father's words. "What's the big box for, Pops?"

He gestured expansively with his other hand. "To hold all the love you guys have given me."

It was one of those storybook moments. I was glad Aaron was there to witness it or I wouldn't have believed it, my sister wouldn't have believed it, no one would've believed it.

It would be several years later, after my father spent three weeks dying, after my sister and I spent eight weeks sifting through the things he left behind, that I would discover my mother's high school photograph, the copy she had given to my father when he was just a boy and she was just a girl, their whole lives ahead of them.

"I'd like to give you a present but I can't find a box big enough to put it in."

How big of a box would I need to hold the things they had given me?

A few days after the box comment, my father slipped into that state somewhere between this world and the next, where he would hover for another two weeks. I didn't know that then; I thought our end was near. But I felt fortunate. Of all the ways our story together could end, this was the best the three of us—my father, my sister and I—could have hoped for. If Nancy hadn't died before he did and if he hadn't quenched his grief with alcohol, if he had stayed well and we all had remained what we had been to one another, we three would never have had the opportunity to live this story of his dying days.

In the days to come, I'd stare at his hollowed face with the slack jaw and cloudy, half-opened eyes, and stroke the flaxen hair off his forehead. "Whatever he did or didn't do," Aaron said to me on one of those long days, "you are who you are because of him."

After witnessing our father's courage in the face of death, after his memorial where we heard the story of his trials during the war, after we unearthed artifacts from his house that offered proof of his love for both of us (a Father's Day card given to him by my mother from my sister as an infant, a poem in his "Record IV" titled "Sam" about "a bundle of sweetness and brightness and fun," a letter opener with a duck's head we had given him with "Sami and Amy, Xmas, 1991" written on it in his careful print) we started to believe what we had always wanted to believe. Our dear ol' dad was a good guy who loved his girls even if we weren't always good at seeing it.

My father died in early May, and at the end of July 2015, my sister and I traveled to Norwalk, the city where our parents' life together—and therefore ours—began. We were meeting Vietch, my father's oldest and closest friend, the man who had known my father when he was just Tommy Hoyt, before he put the "h" in his name and dropped the tail of boyishness. Vietch had known all the players in our family drama—our mother, our stepmother, us. He had not been able to attend the memorial, so as we sat at the bar, Vietch with his cigarette and beer, my sister and I on either side of him with our waters, we recounted the tale that had been told and asked him what he knew about our father's experience as a prisoner of war.

Vietch set his beer down after a long swallow. He was nearing a hard 70, wrinkled and frail looking, but still had the irreverent manner of his youth.

"He chewed what outta what?" He laughed loudly. A guffaw, really. "The only thing your dad chewed in Vietnam was steak."

But what about the story?

"Ah, that was just something your dad told people when he was drunk."

My sister and I looked at each other.

"What the fuck?" one of us said.

Vietch gave a small wave to the woman behind the bar, and she brought him another bottle. "Don't be too hard on your old man," he said, and it took us a moment to realize he was talking about his drinking. "When we were growing up, your grandparents didn't offer us pop, they offered beer. And if you didn't drink it something was wrong with you."

My sister and I knew what he was saying was true. How many times had we heard the same thing from our grandparents when we had declined the offer of a beer?

I thought about how at his memorial service, his old IBM cronies were confused when we told them that our father had died from alcohol-induced liver failure, not cancer. "Huh," they said. "We didn't know it was such a problem. Everybody drank."

"Your dad loved you girls," Vietch said, and even in light of all the untruths, I believed it.

I had no reason to doubt Vietch. Of all the people involved in this story, he had the least motivation to lie. Still, I felt the urge to verify. I Googled "list of air force POWs during Vietnam" and found the Defense POW/MIA Accounting Agency website. My father's name was not on any of the lists. Not on the accounted for, unaccounted for, released or escaped. Nor was he on the list of POWs returned alive on homeofheroes.com. I searched for Hoyt on the national archives page. Nothing. I read about POW phonies on miafacts.org and was encouraged to check the Defense POW/MIA Accounting Agency website I'd already consulted. I also discovered anyone could buy a POW/MIA flag for about 30 bucks.

One thing my father definitely had was 30 bucks.

My sister and I wondered why he would make up such a story.

"Maybe because he's a jackass," I said.

"Maybe because he wanted sympathy," my sister said.

Maybe he felt guilty for having such a cushy time in the war when so many others had suffered. Maybe he had wanted something bad to happen to him so he could see what he was made of. Maybe when nothing did, he had to pretend it had.

But so what if it wasn't true? So what if he was never a prisoner of war, never chewed his way out of a bamboo cage? Aren't we all prisoners of our own wars? Mine, the war between love and truth. All this time I thought I had to choose, thought I had to find the truth—that place between his story and hers, ours and theirs—as though this was where I'd find solid footing. But truth, like love, doesn't live in just one place, in the middle of things. It surrounds and infuses all things.

I thought about what my parents may have expected of me, about whether I was a disappointment. I thought about what I expected of them, about whether I thought they were disappointments. I could almost hear them from beyond, their voices soft but not plaintive: we did the best we could.

By the Thousands

I n the autumn of 2016, as my gathering had just begun, I came across one of my chance objects: my mother's wallet. The wallet was a marvel. By then, it was 40 years old, easy, crumpled and stained, its flap partially torn. But the two snaps were intact. Like my sister and I were intact. We, the lone survivors of this sad and fractured family. Survivors was too strong a word though. Too melodramatic. What was a better one? Members? Remnants? Remains?

We gave the wallet to my mother for Mother's Day when I was in kindergarten. Maybe earlier. We were in Florida by then, just the three of us, living close to my grandparents. It must have been beautiful when it was new, the wallet. Soft, brown suede— cool to the touch—with delicate white stitching. Where would we have found such a thing? My sister would only have been 8 or 9. Had my grandmother taken us shopping? Had we found the wallet at the flea market?

The wallet found its way back to me in the box of stuff that my mother's husband Tom had sent to me after she died. There was another chance object in that box: a Hummel figurine of my mother's. It didn't survive, unfortunately. Tom had packed the box carelessly so that the girl arrived broken. When I first gathered the pieces of what my mother had kept for me, I felt an ache in my core. This small emblem of a happier time, a time that may never have existed so that I missed it all the more keenly.

I had forgotten all about this Hummel figurine, The Apple Tree Girl. She must have lurked in my subconscious when I doodled my Gathering Girl. I drew it, I recalled, after my mother's death. Had she been trying to tell me something, my mother?

My Gathering Girl was similar but not the same. A doppelgänger. The Apple Tree Girl was rosy-cheeked innocence cradled by the branches of a tree forever blooming. She looked carefree. Like everything was right in her world. Nothing bad had ever happened to her. No roots showed and the thing with feathers—hopeful bird!—sang sweetly above her. The Apple Tree Girl looked like putting my hand in the flour canister felt.

But the wallet. When I first opened it soon after her death, it was a painful reminder of what could have been, if only. If only my mother never got sick. If only I knew what to do with her sickness. If only I knew what to do with her. What to do with myself. The first time I opened it, I did so with hesitation, trepidation, longing. It smelled like my mother. Like smoke and perfume. Like my "Mamasita," my pet name for her. "You know that means 'whore' in Spanish, right?" one of my patients would one day tell me. I knew that would have made my mother laugh.

Nearly 20 years later, I opened the wallet again. It still smelled like her. I wasn't as raw, but I still had questions. I still wanted answers. At least clues. I wondered what I may have missed the first time.

Inside I found a poem. "Outlaw" was scrawled on the side of the paper.

```
Nothing I could, in lamb white
   days, that Time would take me
Up to the swallow-thronged loft
   by the shadow of my hand,
In the moon that is always
   rising,
Nor that riding to sleep
I should hear him fly with the
   high fields
And wake to the farm forever fled
   from the childless land,
Oh, as I was young and easy in
   the mercy of his means,
Time held me green and dying
Though I sang in my chains
   like the sea.
```

I had thought a crazy man in prison named Outlaw sent it to our mother when we lived in the trailer.

I read the poem, enchanted by its haunting beauty, then read it again out loud to the last line: "Time held me green and dying though I sang in my chains like the sea." I did some research and learned the poem in my mother's wallet was the last stanza of Dylan Thomas' famous "Fern Hill."

I called my sister. "That poem in mom's wallet. It's by Dylan Thomas!"

"Who's Dylan Thomas?"

A few weeks later, I went to my sister's house. It was Christmastime. Our mother had been dead 16 years. Our father, one. We were trying our best to make family traditions for her youngest son, who was 8 years old. My sister had succeeded in breaking the cycle of estrangement with her children. Her love for them and theirs for her was without question. I couldn't think of what my sister had managed to do with her three kids, and with me, without choking on the sweetness of it, knowing from what sorrow it was born.

While the last batches of cookies baked and my sister went to wrap the remaining presents, I dug through the memory box we put together to remember our father, whose birthday was Christmas Day. The box was a rich, dark mahogany. I opened a small tin filled with his tobacco. One whiff—spicy, almost buttery—and I was in tears, thankful the feelings I often worried were gone were not.

Also in the box were my father's journals. I had glanced at them before, right after he died, but had yet to pore through them. I flipped through the one labeled "Record III." It was sparsely filled, with several blank pages between entries. The entries were mostly quotes from things he read, whole passages he copied down, lists of words and their definitions. And then, between what may have been an original quip about humans and a quote from "The Harrad Experiment," written as if it were an afterthought, a reminder to look something up: Thomas' "Fern Hill."

Why was a mention of "Fern Hill" in my father's journal?

I closed the book and put it back in the box. Went to get my sister. I was nervous and excited and a little scared. "You're not gonna believe this!" I shouted down the hall. She yelled from her bedroom for me not to come in. She was wrapping my gifts. I paced her hallway excitedly. "Fern Hill ... Fern Hill ..."

After Christmas, I pored through my father's journals looking for "Fern Hill." In "Record III," sometime in 1968, before his year in Vietnam, I found the Dylan Thomas poem copied in its entirety. The first line: "Now as I was young and easy under the apple boughs ..."

After the poem, my father wrote this:

"This must surely be Dylan Thomas' purest lyric—one in the line of the great laments for lost innocence, for 'the farm forever fled from the childless land.' I remember that boy and that farm. I remember that boy, as Dylan would say, by the thousands."

I Googled "plagiarism check" and ran his words through three times. Each time, the report was clean. One hundred percent unique. By the thousands, my father surprised me.

The Apple Tree Girl. The Gathering Girl. "Fern Hill." What was I to make of the things I had gathered over the last several years? The connections. The coincidences. Were they clues? Answers? What were my questions?

In both the Hummel figurine and the doodle, the girl and the tree and the bird were the things in common. What was different were the roots. In the figurine, the roots were hidden deep, but they wouldn't be hidden long. In time, we would each "wake to the farm forever fled." The mother would disappear; the father would disappear; that little girl, "young and easy under the apple boughs," would disappear. But to help the girl remember who she once was and from whom she came, to help her see the burdens as gifts and give her the facility to bear them both, the roots would surface even as the fruit was falling, and as the bird—I was sure now—was beckoning.

One more thing. Puissant, I learned, from the Latin root "posse," could also mean "to be able."

The Gathering Ends

It was 2019. My husband, Aaron, and I had moved into the house of discarded things we were continually building on the patch of land that now had—thanks to Aaron's willingness and ability to literally move the earth for me—a south-facing hill.

It had been three years since I began to gather my chance objects and arrange them just so. They seemed to tell a truer story than any I could ever have told on my own. In this new telling, I made peace with what I could. Now could I let the rest go?

I wanted to. I did. But the sense of disconnection—I couldn't seem to shake it.

Perhaps the answer was in the word itself—disconnection. "Dis," a prefix for reversal and removal, implied a previous connection, didn't it? Perhaps this was what I was thinking about when I wrote in my undergraduate philosophy notebook, the one where I pondered harmony consisting of opposing tensions:

"Where then is our origin? Do we have one? Is our search for union leading us to a previous state of completion, when we were one …? It seems an origin must have existed for we cannot strive for something we have not known. We can thus verify our origin by its absence, and by our desire to return to it."

The idea spurred me on. Must a happy origin have existed to explain my desire to find it? I went digging for new evidence, wanting to make sure I hadn't missed anything, wondering all the while what exactly I was expecting to find. And would it ever be enough? Would I ever piece together an image that would satisfy?

Most of Aaron's and my possessions were stored in the loft in the barn. Nothing was in order. I hefted boxes off other boxes and sifted through their contents, looking for that one box my sister hauled across four states after my mother's death. If there were any other clues, any other evidence, I'd find them in that box.

Under a box of empty Mason jars, I found a box of random things. One was my college photo album. It was not what I was after, but I picked it up anyway, thinking it might be fun later to reminisce about those days. Maybe even instructive to sit and ponder what may have possessed the young woman I used to be to write such a passage about origins and desire.

I opened the album absentmindedly and stopped cold. There, tucked neatly in the front, was another photograph of that Christmas family portrait of my entire family—the four of us on the hearth, beneath the felt wreath. I held the photo in my hand and stared at it in eerie disbelief. How had it gotten in there? My college album was not now nor had it ever been in the box from my mother's. At my dead sister-in-law's house, my mother's box was in the dining room for months, while my college album was stored in the hall closet with my other photo albums. The two had never had an opportunity to cross paths. And yet, there it was. Precisely when I was poking around looking for God knows what.

I found the box from my mother's and hauled it and my college album—with the second family photo still tucked inside—down the loft stairs, across the melting snow and into the house. I paged through the old albums that belonged to my mother. Albums that I had paged through countless times as a child and again over the last few years. I looked at them anew to make sure I'd gotten things as right as I could.

I confirmed the first house was once blue. Also, the existence of the next-door neighbor girl I ran away with at age 4. Of my father and me in the pool. Of the blue velour couch and orange bedroom wall. There were several photos of just my mother and me. They looked staged, the taker possibly prodding my mother to pose with her toddling second daughter. They were uninteresting shots and seemed to confirm my feeling of disconnection.

One other photograph stood out, though. I was about 3 years old, standing next to her as she sat in the rocker with the wine-colored cushion. I was looking at the camera and smiling mischievously. She was looking at me with an expression on her face—not stony, not distant. I peered through my magnifying glass. Her expression was undoubtedly loving and even playful. I looked closer at my own face. I had what appeared to be scabs on my forehead and chin. One of my mother's hands—the one with the oval turquoise stone ring she wore up until her death—

reached out for me as though to tug at my sleeve and say: "You can't get away from me, kid."

Next, I took out the second version of the Christmas family portrait, the other one from 1973, the real epic find.

I was half afraid to look at it. What if everything that I remembered—or didn't remember—about my fractured family was wrong? What if, after seeing what it revealed, I would have to dismantle the narrative I'd written once again? Rearrange the pieces all over?

I knew I must look.

It was taken with a different camera, a Polaroid Land, and showed us in a much more flattering arrangement—full-bodied and somewhat centered, though still far from a great picture. I stared and stared, with and without the magnifying glass, not sure if I was relieved or disappointed.

To me, it told the same story as the first photograph, even solidifying my previous read: four beings thrown together, trying their best to look the part, but not quite pulling it off. There were the clashing patterns of my parents' outfits: my father's plaid trousers; my mother's floral print dress. No one was smiling except my sister—that same sweet, dubious smile. My father looked resigned with his cowed eyes and hunched shoulders, while my mother looked confident and defiant. And me, I looked more than bewildered in this one. I looked squirrely. It seemed, even at not quite 2, I sensed the unease beneath the surface of things. What else could I conclude? One thing was certain: We were once at least this, a semblance of a family.

No rush of satisfaction came from this realization.

But why not? There I was, rooted and rooting, my life a surprising unfolding. From the innocence lost, something deeper gained. I had found my way to a home I always hoped I'd find. The place I'd longed for, I now belonged to. I was adrift no longer. Looking back, I got the sense that I was on course the entire time. What more could I want? Couldn't this be enough?

Yes. It absolutely could.

As an undergrad, I spent a semester translating The Homeric Hymn to Demeter, an Ancient Greek myth rich in detail, its symbolism complex. It was the last line I thought of now: "And I shall remember you, and a new song as well."

There was a likelihood, a probability, a semblance, by the obsolete definition, that we were indeed a family, once, upon a time, and that now we were my remembrance of a family. A family perhaps never realized in the way I wanted, the way any of us wanted, but a family—my family—exactly as we were supposed to be.

Epilogue

And so, as I was able, so I have. I've gathered the harvest of our season together. Like the Gathering Girl I salvaged what I could, canning like fruit the stones of peace and love and joy, guilt and hurt and sadness, all into a jar I'll call sorrow. When spring comes again, I'll open the jar and off the stones will fly on the wings of hope to fall like seeds, whole and broken, mended and rent. New roots to grab at our feet and remind us from whom we come and why. We will have the words and the words will be known. Nothing bad will ever happen to us. We will be soft and safe and whole. Our hands forever in the flour canister. Young and easy. Green and dying. We will sing in our chains like the sea.

Acknowledgment of Gifts

This book is, for me, a gift comprised of many gifts given to me by many people over the course of my life. Let's open my big imaginary box and see what's inside.

From my mother: a love of words and an electric typewriter when I was 13 on which to type those words.

From my father: a bound copy when I was 18 of my first collection of words, the incomparable "Shades of Grey" (cf. the "e" in grey to my father's "h" in Thom).

From my sister: boundless patience with my constant questioning and the carting of a box of photographs from Colorado to Alaska to South Dakota and finally, to Ohio.

From my first writing mentor, the late Robert Flanagan: recognition and belief in my words.

From my Ohio State University writing mentors, the late Lee K. Abbott, Michelle Herman, Lee Martin and Bill Roorbach: their collective knowledge on the crafting of words.

From Kathleen English Cadmus: an introduction to the River Teeth Nonfiction Conference and the Ashland University MFA program.

From Joe Mackall: the grenade he dropped on my earlier manuscript, prompting me to ask "What am I trying to write about and why?"

From my Ashland University writing mentors, Steven Harvey, Robert Root, Tom Larson, Bonnie Rough and Kate Hopper: guidance, support and encouragement to take my words to a whole 'nother level.

From Kate Hopper (Your Rightness!): an appreciation for chronology, a prompt that led to a new beginning, and an invitation into the best writing community ever.

From the Fisher Cats (said best writing community ever, you know who you are): the listening to many of the words that have gone into these pages.

From my Tuffies, Chad Miller, Katherine Heintschel and Mark Putney: the reading of nearly all the words that have gone into these pages.

From Publish Her: skilled and loving midwifery that has brought this book to life.

From Doug: forgiveness and a reminder that I was never in this story alone.

And from my husband, last and always most, Aaron Rush: … I'll need a bigger box.

About the Author

Amanda Irene Rush's writing has appeared in Vanderbilt Press' 2008 anthology "The Way We Work," "The Bellevue Literary Review," Brevity's Nonfiction Blog, "The Saturday Evening Post" online magazine, "Peatsmoke" and "Black Fork Review." One of her short stories, "Too Good to Be Forgotten," was nominated in 2022 for the Pushcart Prize. She is an enthusiastic collector of rejections, her first coming from the University of Iowa Press in the late '80s for her aforementioned incomparable collection of poetry, "Shades of Grey." She earned a Bachelor of Arts from Ohio Wesleyan University where she studied Ancient Greek and existentialism. Years later, she earned a Master of Science in nursing from the Ohio State University. Years later still, she earned an MFA in creative nonfiction from Ashland University. A psychiatric nurse practitioner since 2008, she now runs a solo practice in Columbus, Ohio, where she does everything from writing prescriptions to cleaning the toilet. She lives and writes in bucolic Champaign County, Ohio, in a house she and her husband built out of discarded things. She is caretaker to four cats, a dog and a tortoise. You can read more (and listen to some!) of her work at www.amandairush.com. Please join her tens and tens of followers on Twitter @AmandaIrene72.

About the Images

The images in this book include the original drawings, photographs, journal entries and correspondence of the author, and the author's deceased mother and father; the author holds the copyright to these images. The images on pages 125-129 are used with permission from www.abandonedfl.com and copyright holder D. Bulit.

www.ingramcontent.com/pod-product-compliance
Lightning Source LLC
Chambersburg PA
CBHW030358130626
46549CB00004B/1545